Girls wanna have fun!

Fun Fingers, Fancy Feet

Written by Jane Glicksman
Illustrated by Charlene Olexiewicz
Photographs by Ann Bogart

LOWELL HOUSE JUVENILE
LOS ANGELES
NTC/Contemporary Publishing Group

To my mother, and special thanks to Hallie, who cheerfully tried out all my nail designs, and Lois, who assembled many of the crafts

—J.G.

Published by Lowell House
A division of NTC/Contemporary Publishing Group, Inc.
4255 West Touhy Avenue, Lincolnwood (Chicago), Illinois 60712 U.S.A.

Managing Director and Publisher: Jack Artenstein
Director of Publishing Services: Rena Copperman
Editorial Director: Brenda Pope-Ostrow
Project Editor: Amy Downing
Photo Shoot Storyboards: Stacie Chaiken
Nail Artists: Charlene Olexiewicz and Treesha R. Vaux
Hand and Foot Models: Jamie Fredrickson, Shannon Olexiewicz, Emma Pallone, Bryn Sowa, and Bari Sowa
Crafts Artist: Lois Rosen
Designer: Treesha R. Vaux

Library of Congress Catalog Card Number: 99-76523

ISBN: 0-7373-0330-1

Lowell House books can be purchased at special discounts
when ordered in bulk for premiums and special sales.
Contact Customer Service at the address above,
or call 1-800-323-4900.

Printed and bound in the United States of America

RDD 10 9 8 7 6 5 4 3 2 1

Contents

Before You Start

Before you start decorating your fingers and toes with all the fantastic designs shown in this book, you need to make sure your "canvas" is in good condition. That means getting your nails in the best shape possible. You'll begin with the Basic Manicure, which forms the foundation of all the designs here. A manicure is a treatment done on your hands to take care of them. It takes a little time to master, but the end result is worth it.

To give yourself a manicure, here's what you need:

- cotton balls
- nail polish remover (non-acetone is best; acetone nail polish remover emits harsh fumes and is especially drying to nails and cuticles)
- nail clippers or scissors

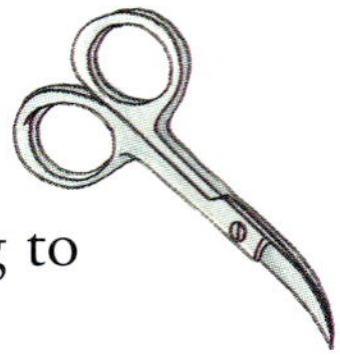

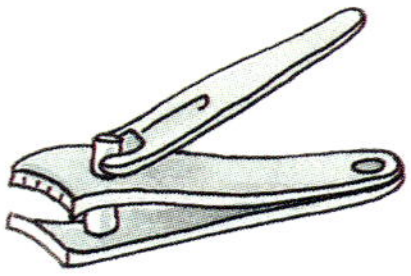

- emery board (stay away from metal nail files, which are hard on your nails)

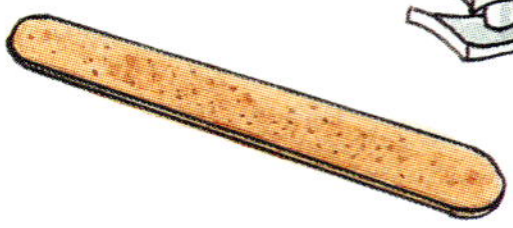

- bowl of warm, soapy water
- nailbrush
- orangewood sticks (available at beauty supply stores and drug stores)

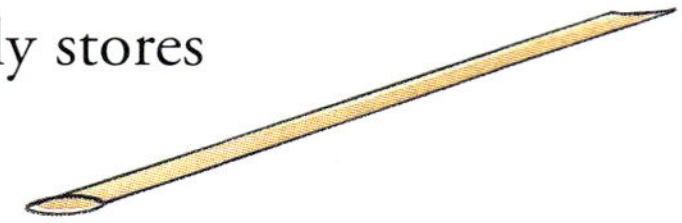

- towel
- clear nail polish (you can use a base coat/top coat combination if you like)
- colored nail polish
- toothpicks (for cleanups)
- hand cream
- cuticle cream or oil (optional)

Nail It Down: The Basic Manicure

Step 1: Remove old polish. Moisten a cotton ball with non-acetone nail polish remover and press on the nail for three or four seconds to dissolve the polish. Wipe upward from the base of the nail to the tip. Use a fresh cotton ball dipped in remover for each nail.

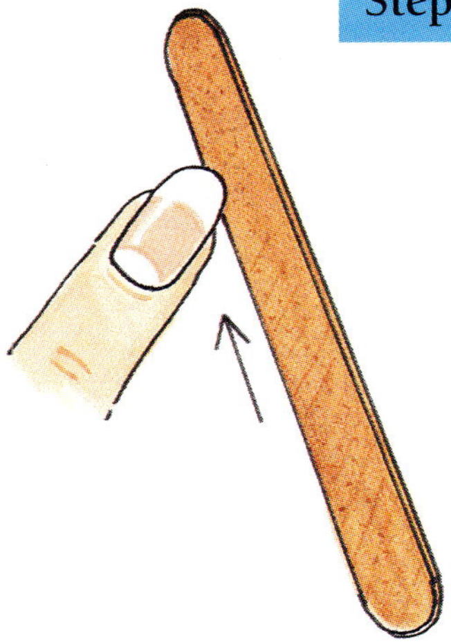

Step 2: Shape and smooth your nails. If your nails are longer than you want them, trim them first with nail clippers or scissors, depending on the shape you would like. (See pages 7and 8 for a few different nail shapes to choose from.) Then file them with an emery board. Holding the file just under the nail, file from one corner of the nail to the center. File in only one direction. If you saw back and forth on your nails, you will split and damage them. Use short strokes, filing first one side, then the other. Don't file too fast—unless you want to start a fire!

Step 3: Soak your hands in warm, soapy water, and use a nailbrush to clean under your nails. For stubborn, caked-in dirt, you can use an orangewood stick to clean under the edges of your nails.

Step 4: Dry your hands and nails with a towel. You are now ready to apply polish, but always shake the bottle a few times before you start. First apply a coat of clear nail polish, or base coat. (Clear polish works as both a base coat and a top coat.) This first coat protects your nails from the dyes of the polish and also helps prevent peeling. When the base coat is completely dry, apply the color of your choice. Or choose a design from this book and begin painting.

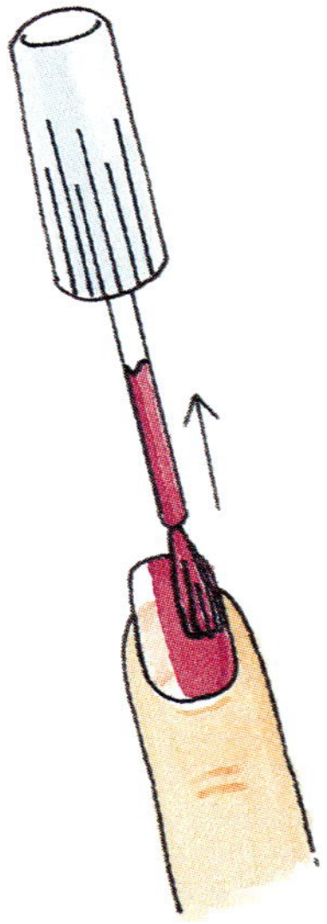

Step 5: Beginning at the center of the nail, apply polish vertically to the entire nail, then run the brush across the top tip of the nail, from one corner of the fingernail to the other. This will seal the polish for a longer-lasting manicure. Wipe away excess polish from cuticles or skin with the edge of a toothpick or an orangewood stick dipped in nail polish remover.

Step 6: When polish is completely dry, brush on the top coat (same clear polish you used for the base coat) to keep nail polish from chipping.

Step 7: After the top coat is dry, apply moisturizing lotion or hand cream to hands and cuticles.

Nail Facts to Know

Clueless on Cuticles?

A cuticle is the skin that grows from your finger to the base of your nail. The cuticle keeps bacteria from entering the space between the nail and the skin. Most nail professionals say "No" to cuticle cutting. Even pushing overgrown cuticles back with an orangewood stick can damage this sensitive area of the nail. So, leave those hardworking cuticles alone! The best thing you can do to keep them soft and supple is to massage cuticle cream or oil into them before you go to bed.

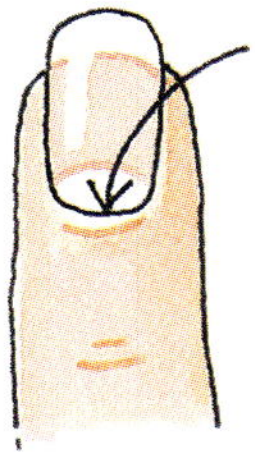

What Nail Shape Is for You?

The hot nail shape of the moment is the "squoval," a short, squared-off oval. Here's how to get it: First trim your nail straight across with nail scissors. Then file the edges slightly to soften the corners.

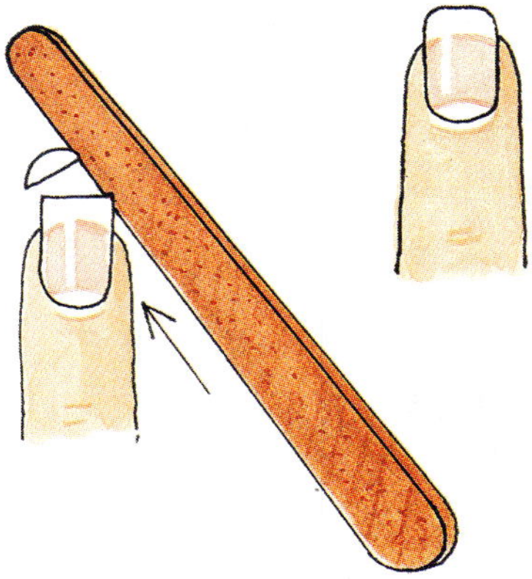

Want to experiment with nail shapes? Use the following guidelines to find the best one for you.

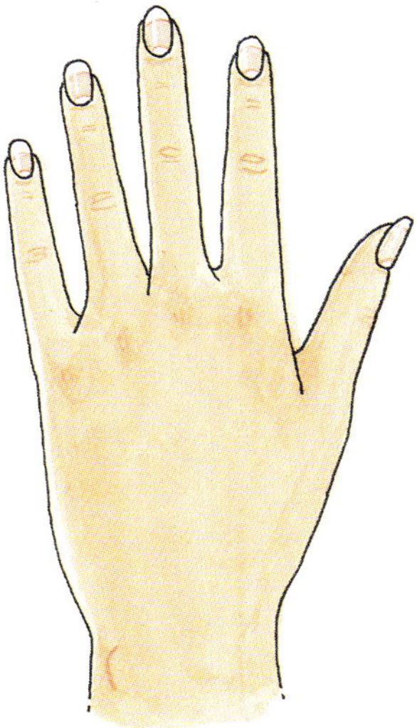

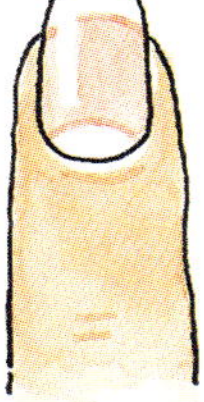

If your hands and fingers are small, and you have oval-shaped cuticles, then oval- or almond-shaped nails are your best bet.

Complement wide hands and nails with longer, squared-off nails.

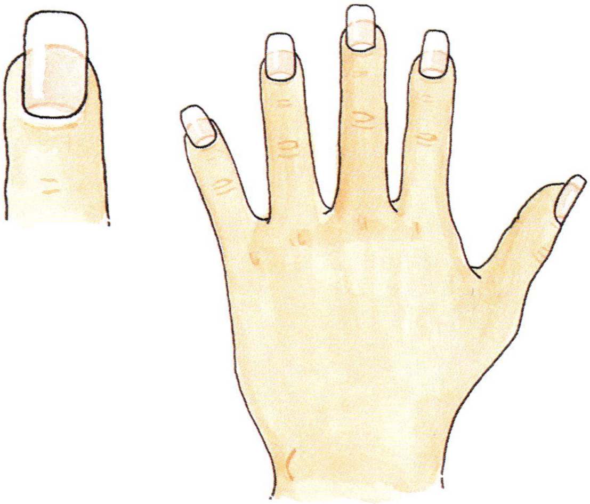

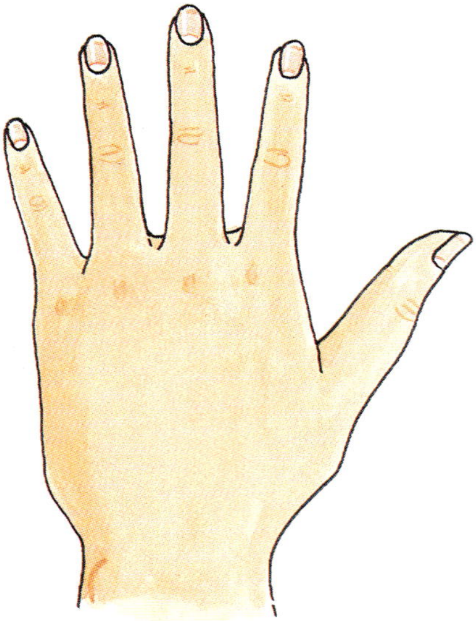

If you want short, rounded nails, first cut them with nail clippers, which naturally give a round shape to the nail. Smooth sides of the nail with an emery board.

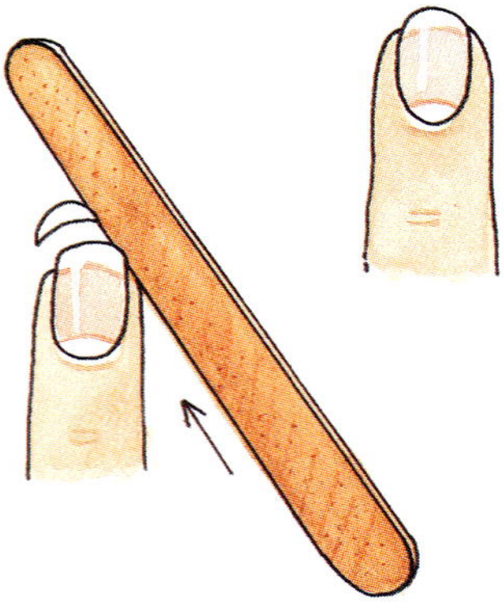

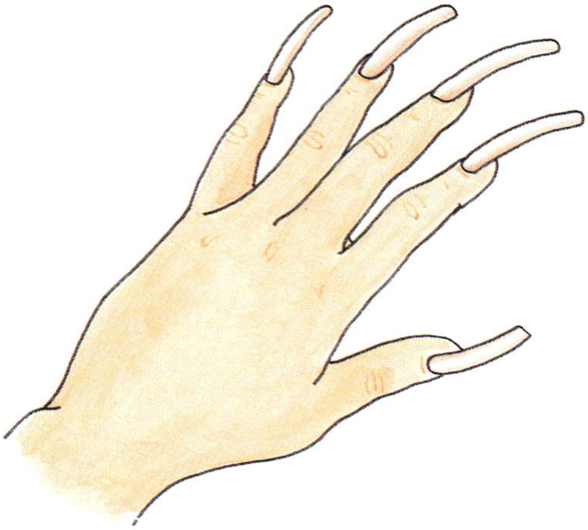

Dragon-lady nails are high maintenance! So, go for the "press-on" type for temporary fun!

Be Kind to Your Hands and Sweet to Your Feet!

Good hygiene is a must! Keep your nails clean with a nailbrush and put cream on your hands and feet daily. Don't forget to cream your cuticles, too. If your cuticles are really ragged, rub a bit of cuticle oil or olive oil onto them before you go to bed. For the softest hands yet, slip on a pair of thin cotton gloves to lock in moisture while you sleep. Treat your feet to some cream as well. Be sure to slather your heels with extra cream.

Milk Manicure

Do you suffer from dry skin and cracked or ragged cuticles? Make 'em drink milk! Milk is loaded with great stuff, such as lactic acid and calcium, to treat you inside and out. Lactic acid, which gently exfoliates, or removes, dead skin, softens even the roughest hands. Calcium is great for building strong bones and teeth, and it does double duty on your nails to keep them healthy. Here's how to give your hands and feet a sinfully rich milk bath: Dissolve 5 tablespoons of powdered milk in 1½ cups of warm water. Soak your hands for about five minutes, then dry and clean your nails and massage your hands. To give your feet the same treatment, double the recipe. Regular milk also works—it's just more expensive.

Tip-Top Toenails

Ingrown toenails can be painful and even get infected. An ingrown toenail occurs when the corner of the nail curves inward and actually grows into the skin at the sides of the nail. To guard against ingrown toenails, cut nails straight across and leave the nail slightly longer than the end of the toe. Smooth nails by filing straight across.

Uncover Your Sole's Soul!

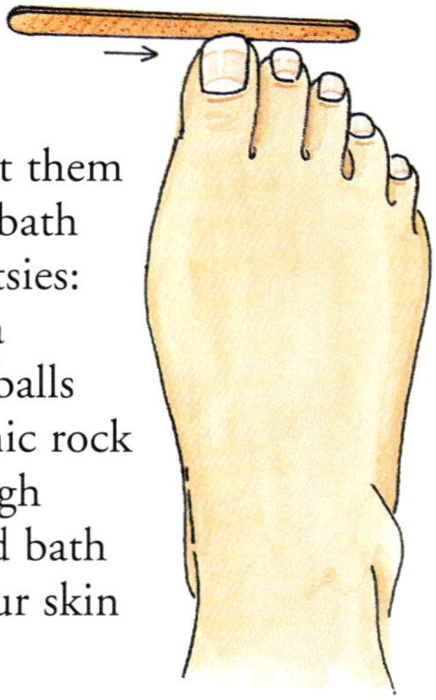

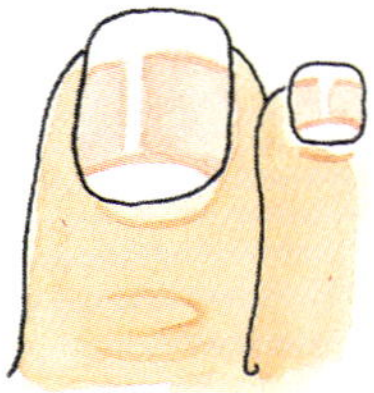

Your feet carry you around every day, so treat them right! Take a few moments in the shower or bath to lavish a bit of extra attention on your tootsies: Lather your feet with soap, then gently rub a pumice stone or loofah across the heels and balls of your feet. A pumice stone is a light volcanic rock used for smoothing rough skin. It is just rough enough to wipe away dead, dry skin. Or, add bath salts to your favorite shower gel to polish your skin until it's smooth as silk!

Here's a spa recipe for a foot soak you can make at home:

Mix together ¼ cup olive oil and the juice of half a lemon in a large pan. Fill the pan with enough warm water to cover the tops of your feet. Soak your feet for 10 minutes. Finish with a salt rub. To do this, rub a cup of sea salt, coarse kosher salt, or Epsom salt over moist skin. Use a pumice stone to massage the salt into your skin. Rinse off with warm water and follow with a rich moisturizer.

Once you've mastered the Basic Manicure, you'll want to try the nail designs in this book. Besides building the supply of nail polish colors listed on the next page, browse your local beauty supply, drug, or art supply store for cool extras, such as nail decals and jewels, stickers, and glitter. Make sure the glitter you use does not have glass in it, because glass can damage your nails. You can also find acrylic "striping" nail art paint at beauty supply stores. Each of these little bottles of nail art paint comes with its own thin brush. One brand to look for is SoEasy Stripe Rite (about $3.50 a bottle).

Use acrylic paints to paint the designs over polished nails. Acrylic paints can be found at any crafts store. Make sure the paint is completely dry before applying new designs, and be sure to apply a clear top coat over your nail art to seal it and keep it from peeling. One of your most important tools will be a good, fine-line artist's brush. Look for the words "liner" or "size 10/0" on the package. You can use a toothpick to apply some designs, but you'll have far less control for detail work.

Nail Art Toolbox

Nail Polishes

The following nail polish colors are essential!

white (the base for many of the designs shown in this book)
red
pink
orange
yellow
blue
green
silver glitter polish
gold glitter polish

Acrylic Paints

These are just the basics—you can mix colors for more variety!

black (most important!)
white
red
blue
yellow

You can create the following colors by mixing the basic-colored paints:

For best results, mix a little of the darker color into the lighter color, one drop at a time. To make colors lighter, add white. To make them darker, add black, one drop at a time.

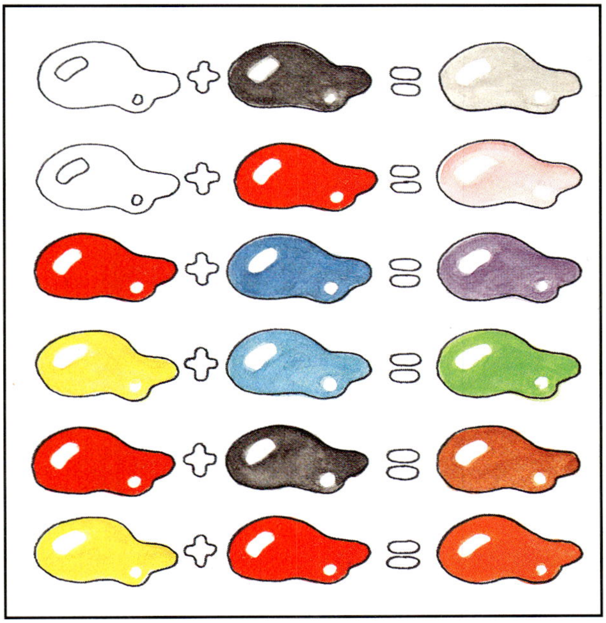

More Essentials

You will need the following for the designs in this book:

- newspaper or paper towels
- fine-line artist's brush
- small glass cup for nail polish remover
- small plastic cup for water
- white ceramic tray or a pad of white palette paper for mixing colors (palette paper trays are available at art supply stores and are quite inexpensive)

Important Tips for Nail Art

- Always work over newspaper or paper towels to catch any spills or drips.
- Never mix nail polish with acrylic paint!
- Wait for nail polish to dry completely before applying a design with acrylic paint. Only use polish to cover the nail. The paints should be used for the designs.
- Clean your brush thoroughly before changing painting mediums or colors. After using nail polish, dip your brush in nail polish remover, then wipe it on a clean paper towel before using acrylic paint. After using acrylic paint, clean your brush in water, then dry it before using nail polish.

- Never store your brush bristles down in a cup of water or nail polish remover, or you'll bend the bristles.
- Keep flat toothpicks on hand to clean up mistakes or clean off wandering polish from cuticles or fingertips.

Design Painting Tips

The following technique will give you more control when painting your designs. Put two or three drops of acrylic paint onto a ceramic tray or palette paper. First dip your fine-line brush in the water, then twirl the brush in the paint, making sure to cover all the bristles. Dip just the point of the brush in the paint again to make a fine point. Now begin your design.

If your paint does not seem to be sticking to the nail, add a dab more water to your paint. (Dipping your brush in the water may add just enough water.)

It is easier to control your brush and draw more precise lines if you stroke upward from the base of the nail. If you are right-handed, begin at the right-hand corner of each nail on your left hand; if you are left-handed, begin your designs at the left-hand corner of each nail on your right hand. You might need a bit of help from a friend when painting your "drawing" hand—and it will be more fun!

To accessorize your dazzling fingertip (and toe-tip!) works of art, we've included designs for a passel of awesome anklets, beautiful bracelets, and rad finger and toe rings that you can create.

Now that you know everything you need to get started on your beautiful nail art, only one thing is missing: friends! Grab a buddy or a bunch of buddies and paint together. You can paint each other's hands for the best look. And as every girl knows, everything is more fun with a pal! Let's get started!

Rainbow Fingers

Paint each fingernail a different color, or follow these simple directions for a lucky rainbow.

You Need

• clear nail polish • red, orange, yellow, green, dark blue, purple, and light blue acrylic paints • white ceramic tray or palette paper • fine-line artist's brush • plastic cup of water

Directions

1 Brush on a clear base coat. Let dry completely.

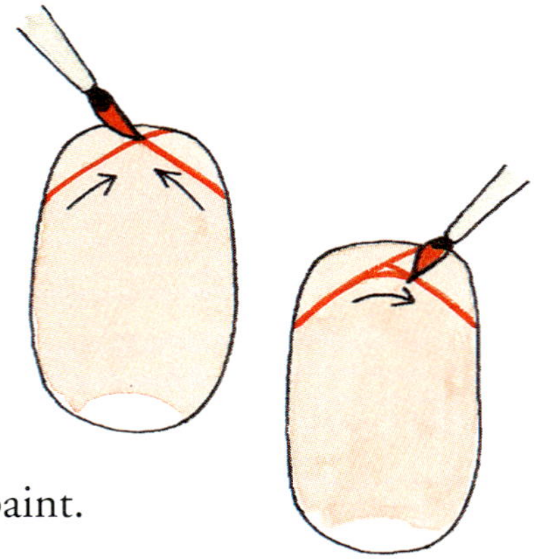

2 Put two or three small drops of red paint on your tray or palette paper. Twirl the brush in the paint. Brush a diagonal stripe from the upper left edge of the nail up to the tip, as shown. Bring another line from the other side of the nail to meet the first line, making an upside-down *V,* as shown. Make a third line rounding off the point of the *V* into an arch. Fill in the nail tip with red paint. Clean your brush.

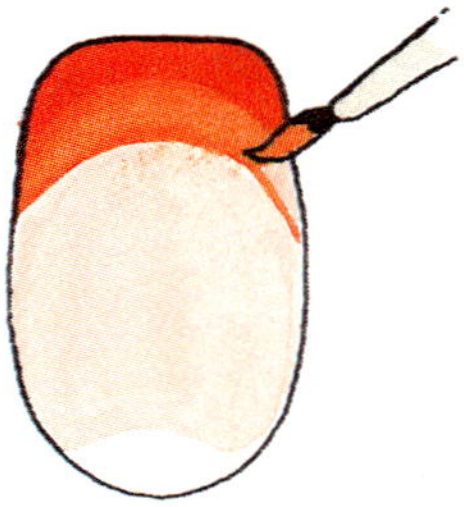

3 Repeat Step 2 to make an orange arch just below the red one. Clean your brush.

4 Repeat the above steps with yellow, green, dark blue, purple, and light blue, in that order, cleaning your brush between colors.

5 Finish with a clear top coat.

Cloud Toes

A perfect design to go with your Rainbow Fingers.

You Need

• clear nail polish • blue and white acrylic paints • fine-line artist's brush
• plastic cup of water • white ceramic tray or palette paper

Directions

1. Brush on a clear base coat. Let dry completely. Apply two coats of blue acrylic paint, letting each coat dry completely. Clean your brush.

2. Put three or four drops of white acrylic paint on your tray or palette paper to form one large drop. Dip your fine-line brush in the water, then twirl the brush in the paint. Starting with your little toe, draw a tiny circle, then fill it in. Draw a slightly larger circle overlapping the first one, and fill it in to make a cloud.

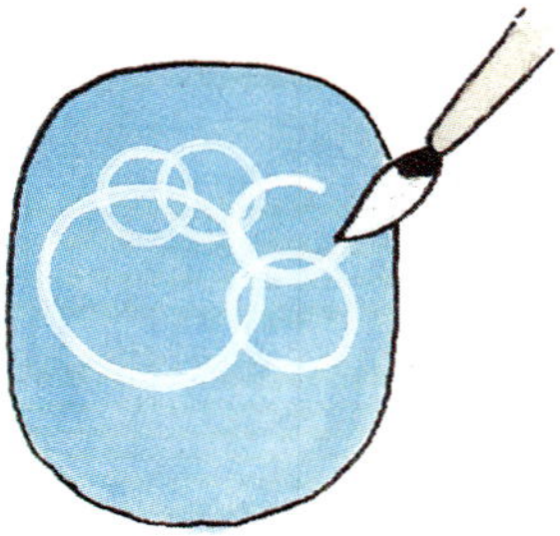

3. Continue as shown with the rest of your toenails. You can vary your design by altering the shapes of your circles and the number of circles or ovals, depending on how much room you have on your nails.

4 When your designs are completely dry, finish with a clear top coat.

Pet Pals

Have a pet or favorite animal? You can take it with you with these paw prints!

You Need

• clear nail polish • white and black acrylic paints • fine-line artist's brush • plastic cup of water • white ceramic tray or palette paper

Directions

1. Brush on a clear base coat. Let it dry, then apply two coats of white acrylic paint to every other finger. Clean your brush, then apply two coats of black acrylic paint on the other fingers. Let your nails dry completely.

2. Put three drops of black acrylic paint on the tray or palette paper to form one large drop. Dip your fine-line brush in the water, then roll the brush in the paint. Starting on one of the white nails, draw a horizontal oval. The top of the oval should be just below the halfway point on your nail. Fill in the oval with paint.

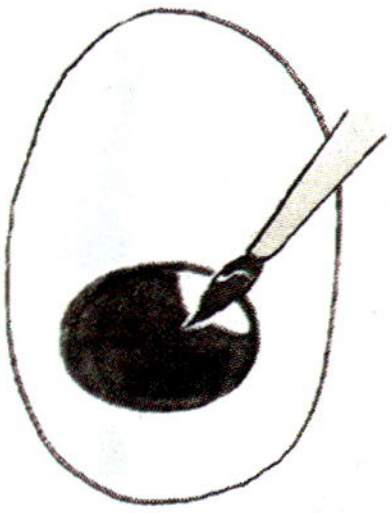

3. Add a half-circle to the top middle portion of your oval. Fill it in with paint. Begin the first toe pad at the top left side of your paw pad. Make a dot. Add the second one right next to the "bump" of the oval. Add the third and fourth toes on the other side, as shown.

4. After cleaning your brush, repeat Steps 2 and 3 with white paint on the black nails. When the paint is completely dry, brush on a clear top coat.

Popsicle® Stick Pet Pals Bracelet

Make a real animal or create your own species!

You Need

• pencil • ruler • wooden craft sticks (½ inch wide) • scissors • sandpaper • phone book • hammer and nail • thin colored markers or watercolor crayons • 10-inch piece of yarn • accessories: black or brown 10-mm-size pom-poms, red felt triangles, black chenille stems (pipe cleaners) • craft glue

Directions

1. Draw a line about 1½ inches from the top of a craft stick. With a parent's help, score the line with scissors.
2. Break the stick along the scored line. Smooth with sandpaper.
3. Lay the flat stick on top of an old phone book. With a parent's help, poke a hole at the top using a hammer and nail.

4. Now, what's your favorite animal? Use your markers or crayons to decorate the front and back of your craft stick. Make up your own creature, and, if you'd like, accessorize it with tiny sequins, cotton wool, or fabric.

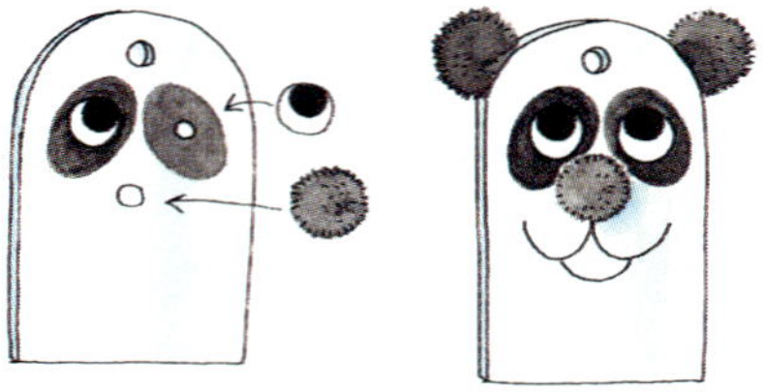

5. Make as many creatures as you'd like, then string them on your piece of yarn. Tie it around your wrist, and cut off the excess yarn.

Little Mouse Ring

You'll want to take this little "pet" everywhere—it's so cute!

You Need

• craft glue • two 10-mm-size white pom-poms • 1 ¾-inch gray pom-pom • 5-mm-size pink pom-pom • two 6-mm-size wiggly eyes (available at craft or art supply stores) • tweezers (optional) • small strip of red felt • 4-inch strip of ⅜ inch wide stretch elastic • scissors • needle and thread • metal clamp (optional)

Directions

1. Glue a white pom-pom on either side of the gray pom-pom for the mouse's ears, as shown.

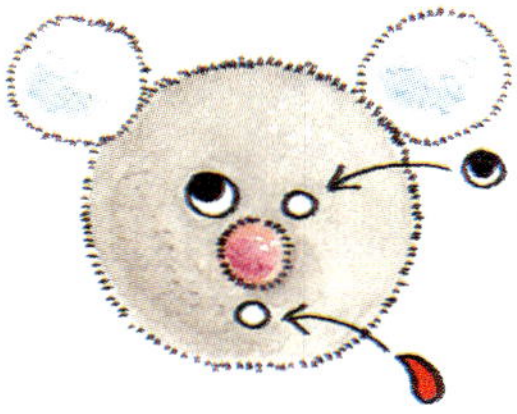

2. Glue the pink pom-pom in the center of the gray pom-pom for the nose.

3. Glue the wiggly eyes in place, on either side of the nose. (You might need tweezers to pick up the tiny eyes.)

4. Glue the strip of red felt in place for the tongue, as shown.

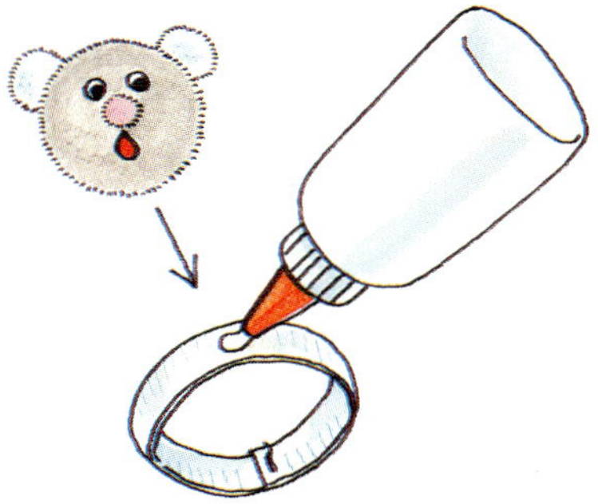

5. Wrap the elastic around your finger to make sure it will fit. (It should be a bit small, as the elastic will stretch.) Trim the excess, then sew the ends of the elastic together with a needle and thread, or glue together, keeping a metal clamp on the glued parts until completely dry.

6 Put a dab of glue on the center of your elastic strip. Put another dab of glue on the back of your gray pom-pom mouse. Press the mouse onto your elastic. Let dry.

Go Safari!

Bring the jungle closer to home with this wild and woolly zebra design.

You Need

• clear nail polish • white and black acrylic paints • fine-line artist's brush • plastic cup of water • white ceramic tray or palette paper

Directions

1 Brush on a clear base coat. Let dry completely.

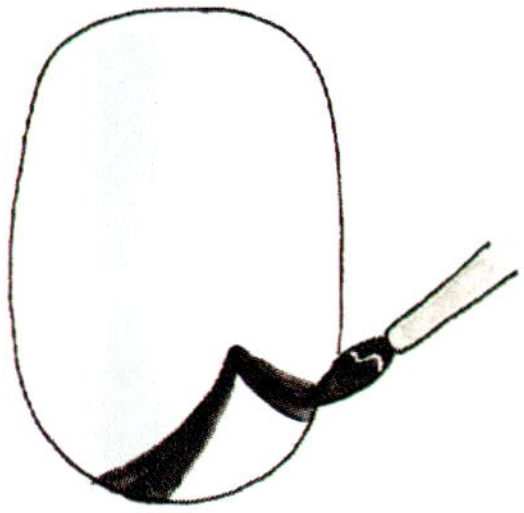

2 Apply two coats of white paint, allowing each coat to dry completely. Clean your brush. Put two or three small drops of black paint on your tray or palette paper. Dip your fine-line brush in the water, then roll the brush in the paint. Beginning at either the lower right- or left-hand corner of your nail, paint an upside-down *V,* as shown.

3 Leaving a bit of white space in between, paint more black stripes going up the length of your nail, as shown. Let dry. Finish with a clear top coat.

Tiger Toes

Your feet will look tiger-ific with this sleek and cool tiger pattern.

You Need

• clear nail polish • yellow and black acrylic paints • fine-line artist's brush • plastic cup of water • white ceramic tray or palette paper

Directions

1. Brush on a clear base coat. Let dry completely. Apply two coats of yellow acrylic paint, allowing each coat to dry completely. Clean your brush.

2. Put two or three small drops of black paint on your tray or palette paper. Dip your fine-line brush in the water, then roll the brush in the paint. Load the tip of your brush with paint, then drop a dab on the top left-hand corner of your nail. To make a horizontal "teardrop" shape, place your brush in the center of the dab of paint, then drag gently to the side.

3. Continue making tiger stripes on your nail, as shown. When your design is completely dry, finish with a clear top coat.

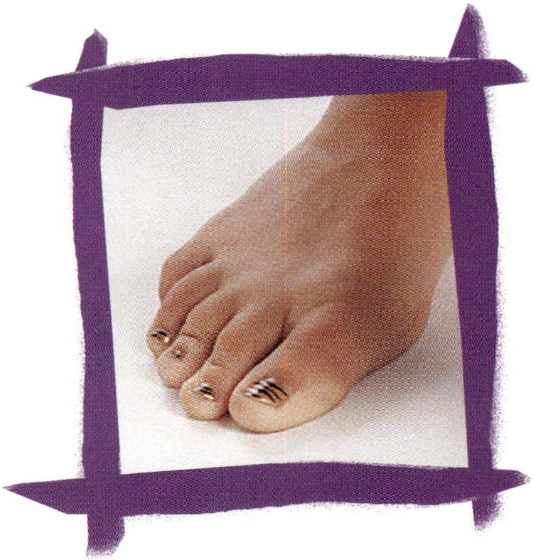

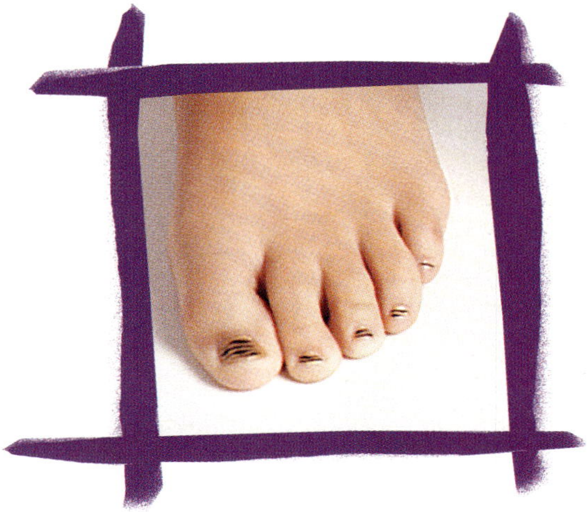

Sweetheart Nails

Romance is in the air with these sweet little hearts.

You Need

• clear nail polish • pink nail polish • red acrylic paint
• white ceramic tray or palette paper • fine-line artist's brush • plastic cup of water

Directions

1. Brush on a clear base coat. Let dry completely.

2. Apply two coats of pink polish. Let dry completely.

3. Put three small drops of red paint on your tray or palette paper. Dip your fine-line brush in the water, then twirl it in the paint. Starting from the lower center of your nail, paint a line, as shown.

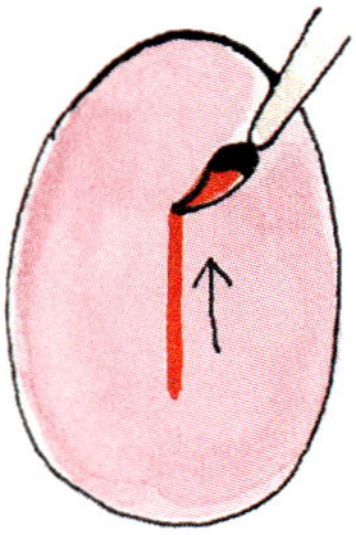

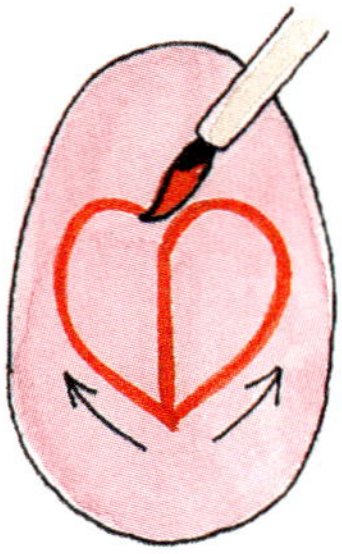

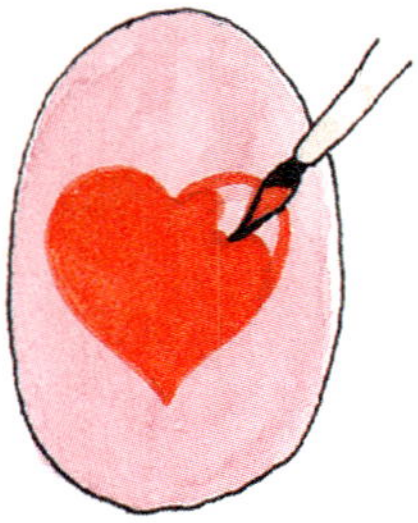

4. Using the line as your reference point, paint the curves of your heart shape, as shown. Fill in with paint. When your design is dry, apply a clear top coat.

Little Hearts Bracelet

Complete your love-ly look with a charming bracelet.

You Need

• piece of air-dry modeling clay • rolling pin • butter knife • sandpaper • paintbrush • various colors of acrylic paints • acrylic sealer • poster board cut to 8 inches by 2 inches • white or craft glue • hole punch • two red or white shoelaces • scissors

Directions

1. Roll out the clay with a rolling pin. With the butter knife, cut out two or three hearts. Let hearts dry.

2. Smooth edges of hearts with sandpaper.

3. Paint your hearts. Don't stop at red! Be wild—paint in stripes or polka dots, if desired. When paint is dry, apply a coat of sealer to both sides of the heart. Let dry completely.

4. With scissors, round off the corners of the poster board piece. Glue the hearts onto the poster board and let dry.

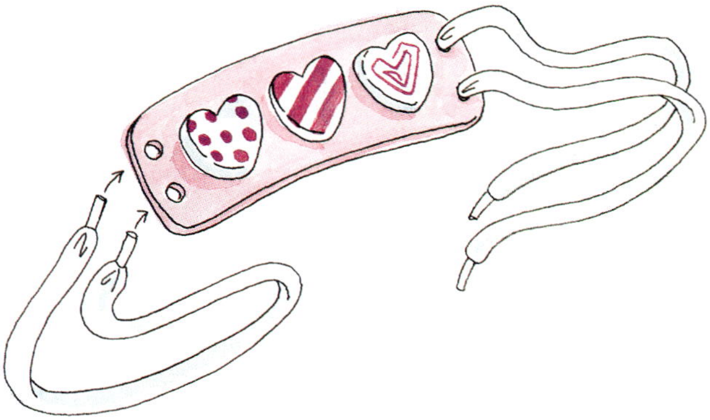

5 Use a hole punch to punch two holes at each end of your poster board bracelet. Thread one shoelace through each hole and tie around your wrist to fasten bracelet. Trim off any extra shoelace.

Lucky Clover Toes

Catch the spirit of the Irish with this adorable look, perfect for St. Patrick's Day.

You Need

• clear nail polish • green and white acrylic paints
• white ceramic tray or palette paper • fine-line artist's brush
• plastic cup of water

Directions

1. Brush on a clear base coat. Let dry completely. Brush on two coats of white acrylic paint, allowing each coat to dry completely.

2. Put two or three small drops of green acrylic paint on your tray or palette paper. Dip your fine-line brush in the water, then roll the brush in the paint. Starting at the center of the nail, make a small circle, as shown. Fill in with paint.

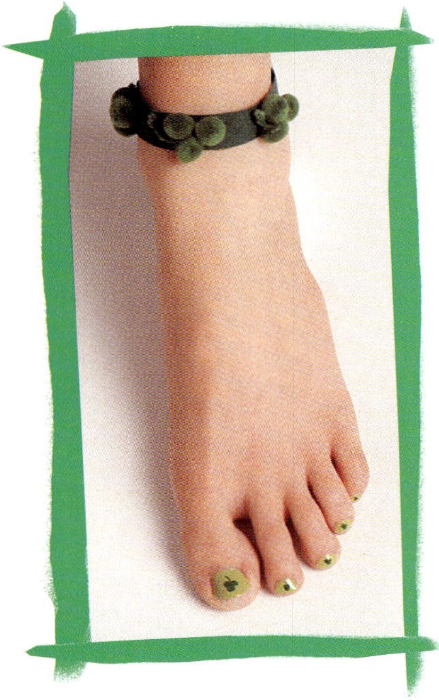

3. Make two more circles, slightly lower, on either side of the first circle, as shown. From the middle circles, stroke downward to make the stem of the clover, as shown. Let design dry.

4. Finish with a clear top coat.

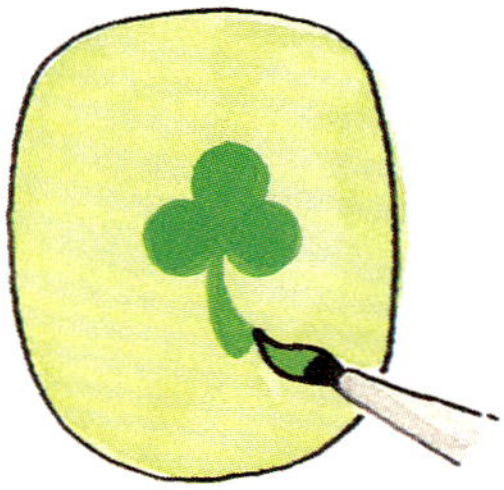

St. Patrick's Pom-pom Anklet

This cute anklet also makes a great bracelet.

You Need

• scissors • ruler • 5/8-inch-wide white or light green ribbon
• white or craft glue • nine 10-mm-size green pom-poms
• green pipe cleaner

Directions

1 Cut 18 inches of the ribbon, enough to tie around your ankle. (Cut about 12 inches for a bracelet.)

2 Glue three pom-poms at the center of the ribbon, as shown. Snip off a ½-inch piece of pipe cleaner. Glue it to the base of your pom-pom clover for a stem.

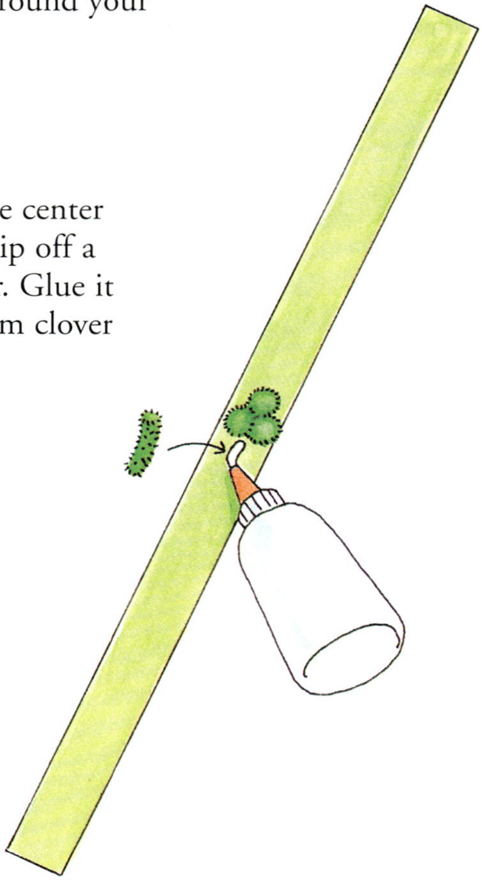

3 Add two more groups of pom-poms and stems on either side of the first group. To secure, tie it around your ankle (or wrist). Trim the excess ribbon.

Flowery Friendship Bracelet

You can make a super sunflower here, or use the instructions as a guide to create any colored flowers you wish!

You Need

• 24 inches of string or plastic cord • craft or white glue
• six yellow beads • black bead • three green beads • scissors

Directions

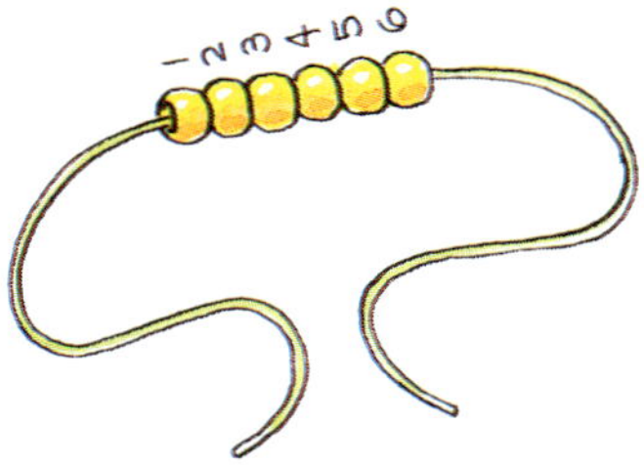

1. Coat the ends of your string with glue to keep them from unraveling. (You don't have to do this if you are using plastic cord.)

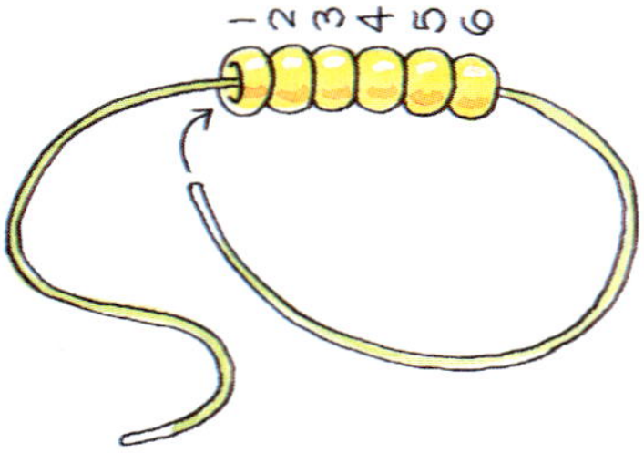

2. String your six yellow beads onto the string or cord and push them to the center. Bring the string or cord around and slide through bead number 1. Tighten.

3. String the black bead and push it to the center of your flower. Feed the string or cord back through bead number 4, as shown. Tighten.

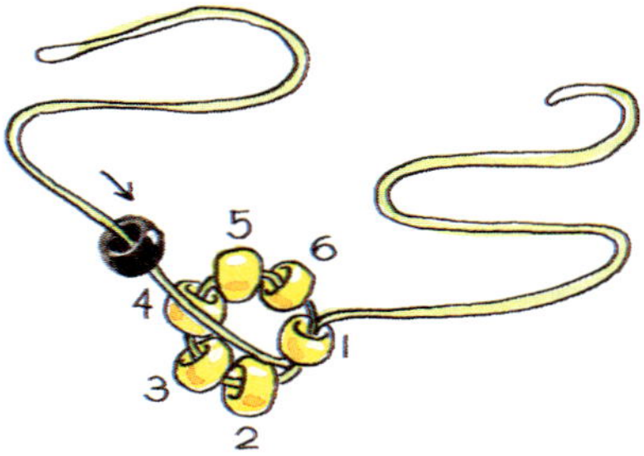

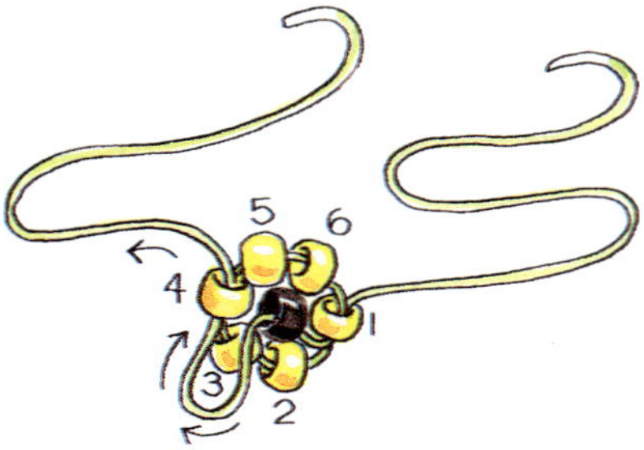

4. Tie a knot on both sides of your flower. String a green bead onto each side. Tie another knot on both sides to secure the beads.

5. Tie another knot about an inch from the first knot on both sides of your string or cord. Slide a green bead on each side and knot again, as shown. Tie the bracelet on your wrist and trim off any excess string or cord.

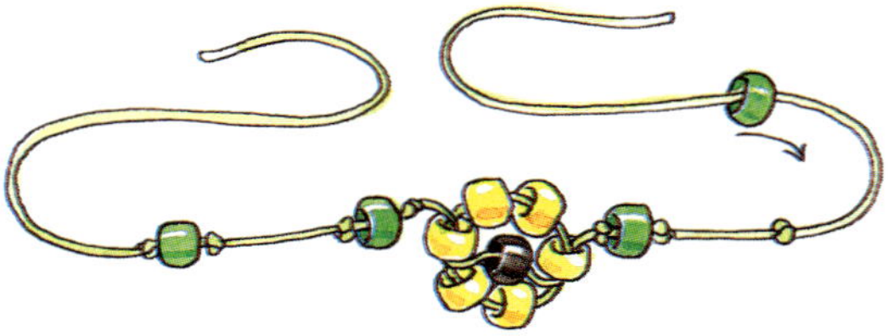

Sunflower Power

Make a bouquet of spring flowers on your nails to jazz up any warm-weather outfit.

You Need

• clear nail polish • light green, brown, and yellow acrylic paints
• white ceramic tray or palette paper • fine-line artist's brush • plastic cup of water

Directions

1. Brush on a clear base coat. Let dry completely. Put two small drops of light green acrylic paint on your tray or palette paper. Dip your fine-line brush in the water, then roll the brush in the paint. Paint a coat of light green acrylic paint on your nails and allow to dry. Clean your brush.

2. Put two small drops of brown acrylic paint on your tray or palette paper. Dip your brush in the water, then roll the brush in the paint. Paint a circle in the center of each nail and fill with paint. Let dry. Clean your brush.

3. Put three drops of yellow acrylic paint on your tray or palette paper. Dip your brush in the water, then twirl it in the paint to cover the bristles completely. Paint five or six petals around the brown center as if you were drawing in the rays of a star.

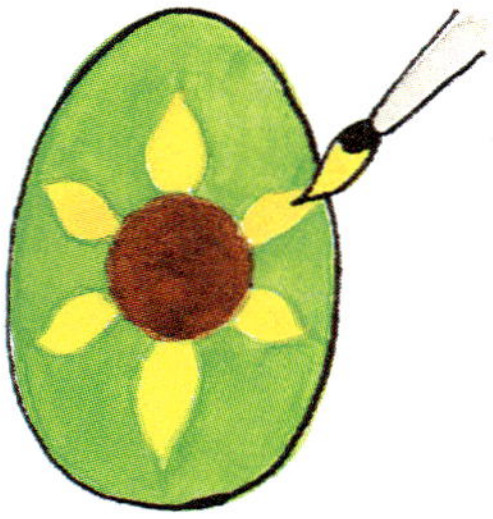

4. Now fill in the spaces around your "star" with smaller petals. Dab a few yellow dots on the brown circle.

5 Put two more drops of yellow paint on your tray or palette paper. Clean your brush, then add a drop of brown. Wet your brush, then mix the brown with the yellow. Use the darkened yellow to shade in some more sunflower petals.

6 When your flower is dry, finish with a clear top coat.

Spring Swirl

Celebrate spring with pastel colors and this unusual abstract design.

You Need

• clear nail polish • yellow, blue, white, and pink acrylic paints
• fine-line artist's brush • plastic cup of water

Directions

1. Brush on a clear base coat. Let dry completely. Brush on two coats of yellow acrylic paint, allowing each coat to dry. Clean your brush.

2. Put a couple drops of the paints on your tray or palette paper. With the fine-line brush, drop a dab of blue paint on the center of your nail. Dip your brush in the center of your drop. Gently drag the brush through the color to make an abstract design. Let dry completely. Clean your brush.

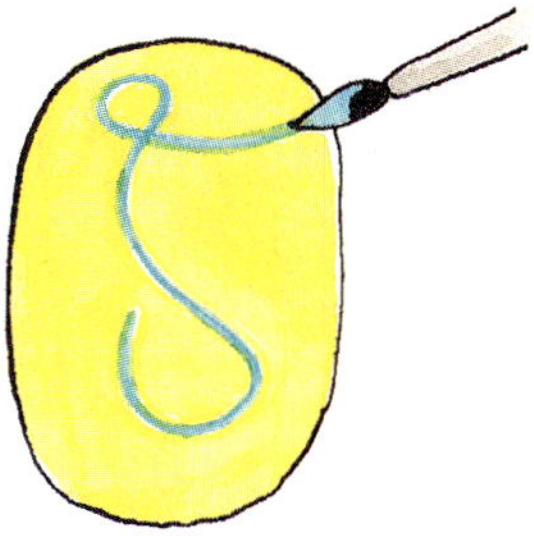

3. Repeat Step 2 with the remaining paint colors, allowing each color to dry completely. Finish with a clear top coat.

Unfurl Your Swirl!

Try this pattern on red nails or nude nails. Experiment with your colors. Try moving your brush in a feathered motion for a pattern that looks like a peacock feather!

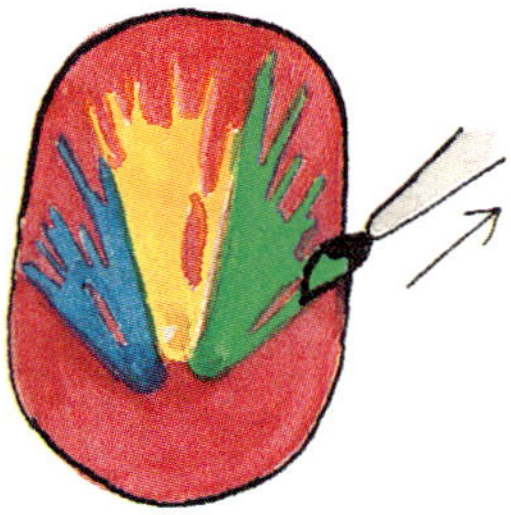

Henna Sun

Washable markers make great henna imitations.

You Need

- plastic cap from gallon milk or juice jug, about 1 ½ inches in diameter
- red-brown washable fine-tip marker (black works, too)

Directions

1. Lay the cap on top of your hand. With the marker, trace a circle around the edge of the cap.

2. Draw a dot at the 12 o'clock, 3 o'clock, 6 o'clock, and 9 o'clock positions just outside the outline of your sun.

3. Draw three squiggly lines in between each dot, as shown. If you like, draw a happy face inside. Continue decorating as you wish. Your "henna" sun will last until your next shower!

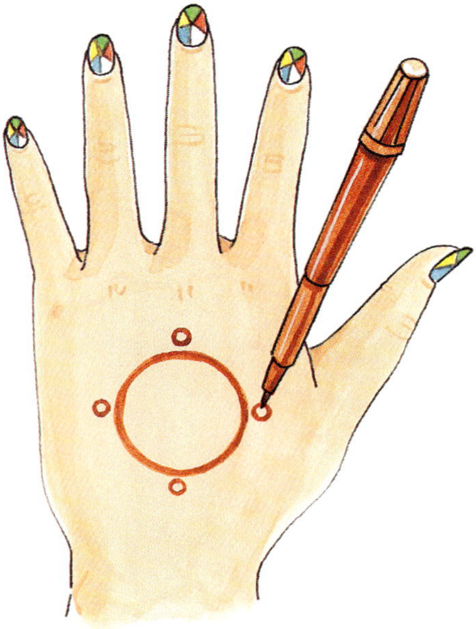

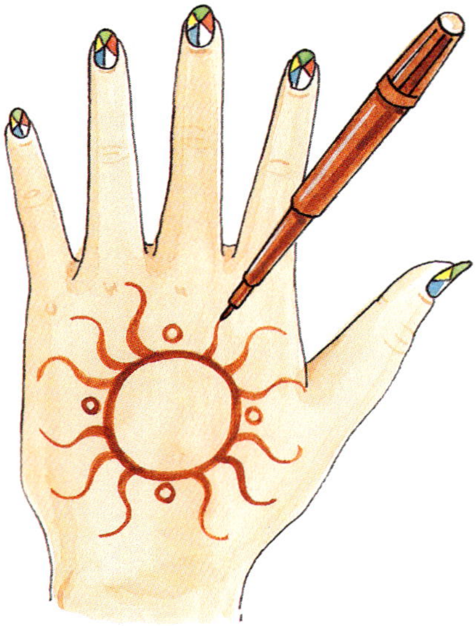

Beach Ball Fingers

What a fun look for those hot summer days at the beach, lake, or pool!

You Need

• clear nail polish • white, black, green, red, blue, and yellow acrylic paints • fine-line artist's brush • plastic cup of water • white ceramic tray or palette paper

Directions

1. Brush on a clear base coat. Let dry completely. Apply two coats of white acrylic paint, letting each coat dry completely. Clean your brush.

2. Put two small drops of black acrylic paint on your tray or palette paper. Dip your fine-line brush in the water, then roll the brush in the paint. Starting from a point at the center of your nail, make a *Y,* as shown. Stroke upward to make the "arms" of the *Y,* then stroke downward to make the stem. Starting from the center again, draw two more diagonal lines, facing downward, as shown. Clean your brush.

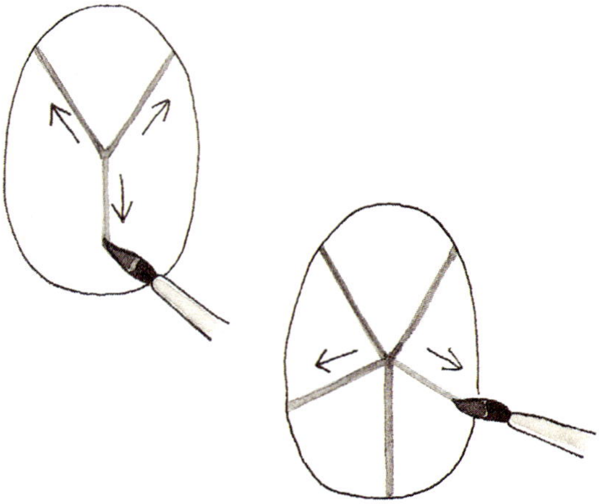

3. Set two small drops of green acrylic paint on your tray or palette paper. Dip your fine-line brush in water, then twirl it in the paint. Fill in the top triangle. Let the paint dry, and clean your brush.

4 Set two small drops of red acrylic paint or your tray or palette paper. Dip your brush in water, then in the paint. Fill in the triangle just to the right of the green one. Leave the triangle next to the red one white. Continue in this manner with the blue and yellow.

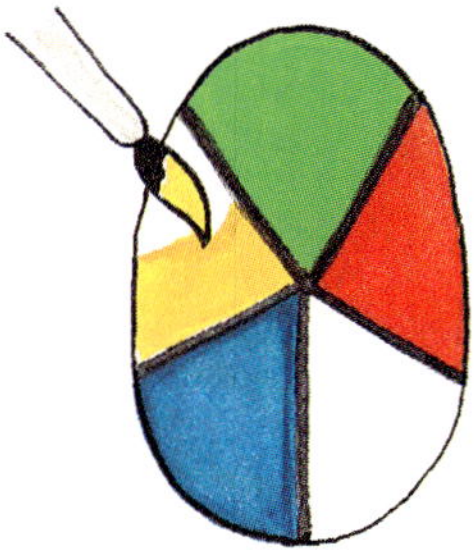

5 When all the paint is dry, finish with a clear top coat.

Patriotic Toes

A Fourth of July favorite!

You Need

• clear nail polish • white, blue, and red acrylic paints • fine-line artist's brush • plastic cup of water • white ceramic tray or palette paper

Directions

1. Brush on a clear base coat. Let dry completely. Apply two coats of white acrylic paint, allowing each coat to dry. Clean your brush.

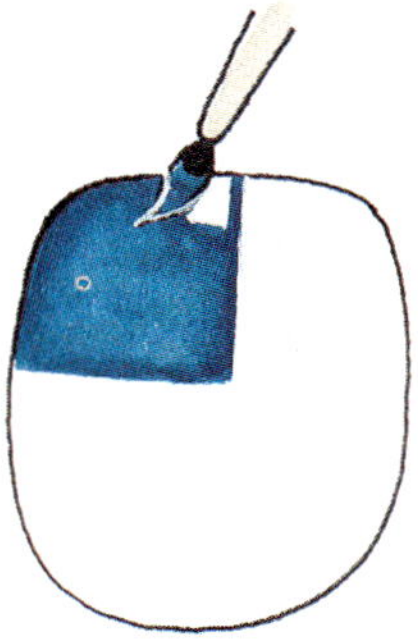

2. Put two or three small drops of blue acrylic paint on your tray or palette paper. Dip your fine-line brush in the water, then roll the brush in the paint, making sure to cover all the bristles. At the upper left-hand corner of your toenail, make a small square, as shown. Let dry. Clean your brush.

3. Put two or three small drops of red acrylic paint on your tray or palette paper. Dip your brush in water, then starting from the top right side of the blue square, brush horizontal stripes across your nail, as shown. Clean your brush thoroughly.

4. Set a small drop of white paint on your tray or palette paper. Dip your fine-line brush into the water, then the paint. Make tiny dots for stars on your blue square. When your design is completely dry, cover with a clear top coat.

Scrunchie Anklet

Scrunchies are not just for hair! Use some colorful fabric and elastic to make a kicky anklet to show off your beautifully manicured toes!

You Need

• $16\frac{1}{2}$ x 5-inch rectangle of red, white, or blue cotton material • needle and thread • one small and one large safety pin • 10-inch piece of $\frac{1}{4}$-inch- or $\frac{3}{8}$-inch-wide elastic • four or five small American flag toothpicks • wire cutters • strong craft glue • red, white, and/or blue buttons, beads, or sequins

Directions

1. Fold the cotton material together lengthwise, with the front side of the fabric on the inside.

2. Stitch the longer edge together, about $\frac{1}{2}$ inch from the edge. You might need a parent to help with this step.

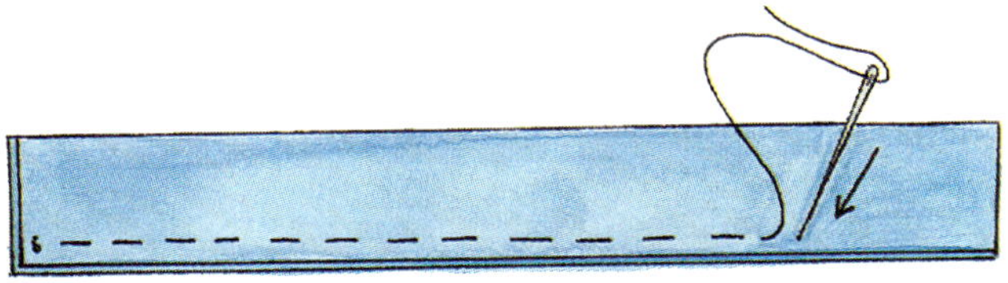

3. Turn the tube inside out. (The front side of your fabric should be on the outside.) You should now have a long tube $16\frac{1}{4}$ inches x 2 inches.

4. Using the small safety pin, attach one end of the elastic to one end of the tube. Attach the large safety pin to the other end of the elastic. Thread it through the tube.

5 Take both ends of the elastic and tie a knot, leaving about ½ inch extra elastic beyond the knot. Fold over the raw edges of the fabric, tuck the elastic inside, and hand sew the two sides of the fabric together to finish the tube.

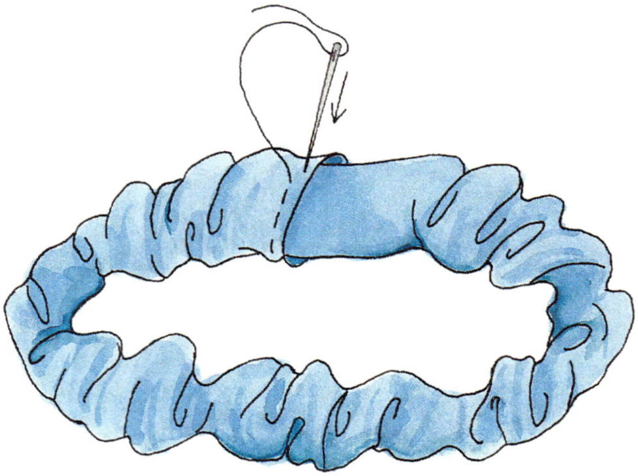

6 To match your Patriotic Toes, take four or five small American flag toothpicks, which you will attach to the scrunchie. (You may want to cut the bottoms of the toothpicks off with wire cutters.) Glue the flags and the buttons, beads, or sequins onto the scrunchie. You should use only a drop of glue for each item. This way, the decorations won't fall off when you stretch the scrunchie to get it on. Allow the glue to dry overnight before wearing.

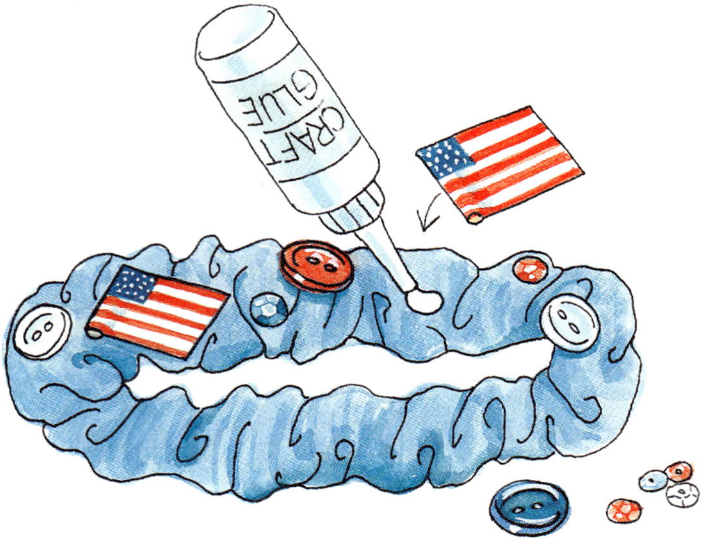

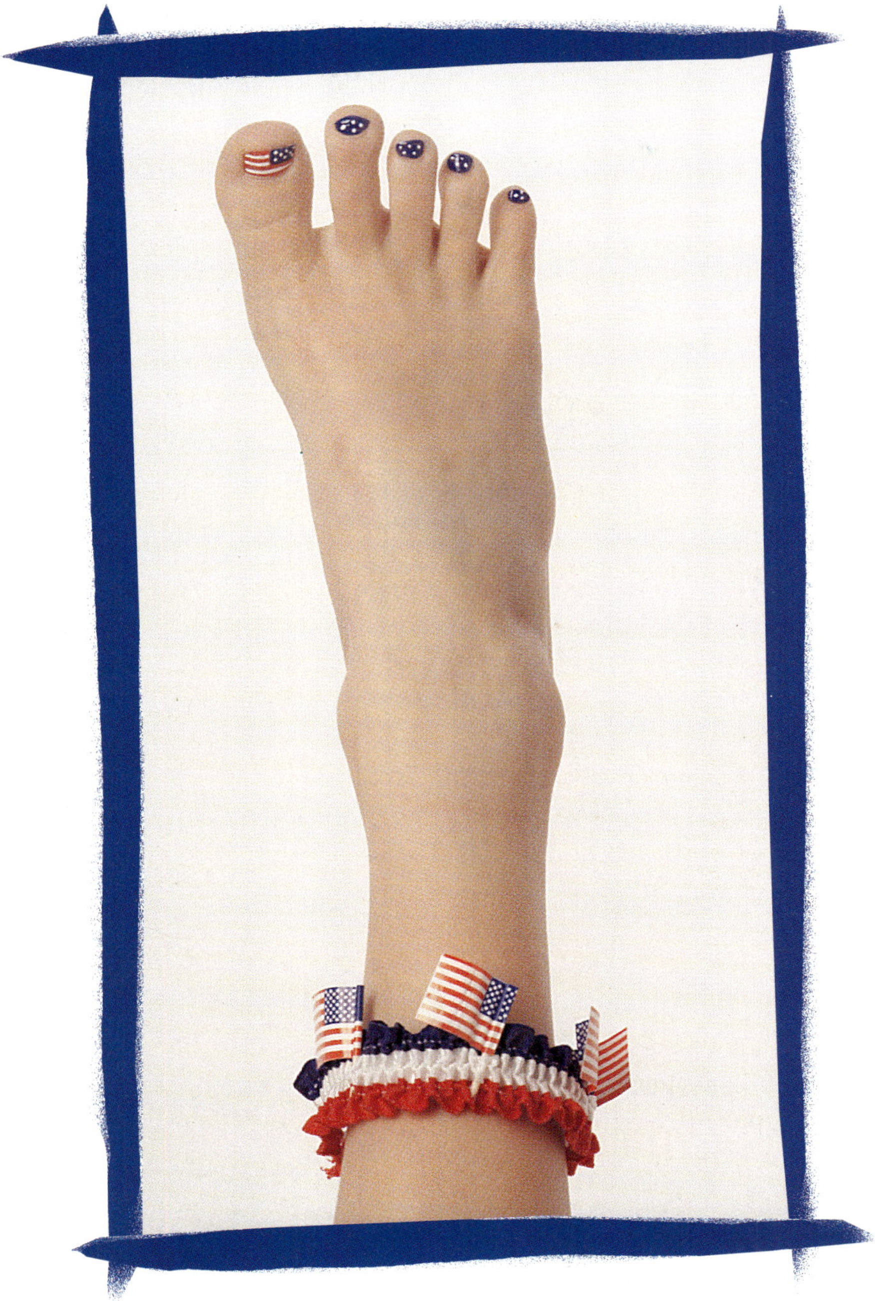

Candy Corn Fingers

They look good enough to eat!

You Need

• clear nail polish • orange nail polish • yellow and white acrylic paints
• white ceramic tray or palette paper • fine-line artist's brush
• plastic cup of water

Directions

1. Brush on a clear base coat. Let dry completely.

2. Brush on two coats of orange nail polish, allowing each coat to dry.

3. Put two or three small drops of yellow paint on your tray or palette paper. Dip your fine-line brush in the water, then the paint. Brush a diagonal stripe from the middle corner of the nail up to the tip on the opposite side, as shown. Fill in with paint. Bring another line from the other side of the nail to meet the first line, making an upside-down *V,* as shown. Fill in the top portion of the nail with paint. (You may need two coats to cover the orange!) Clean your brush in the cup of water.

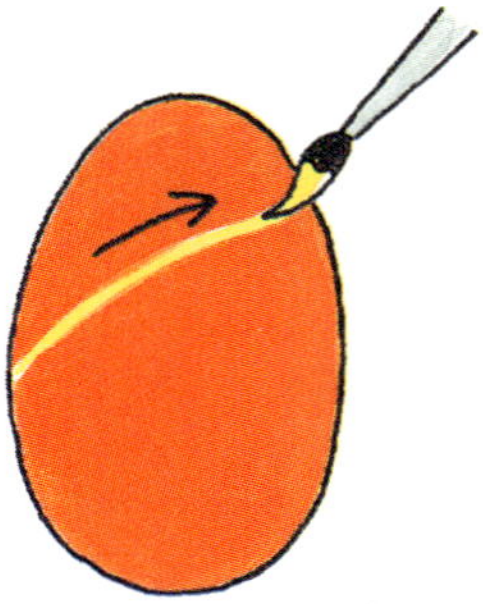

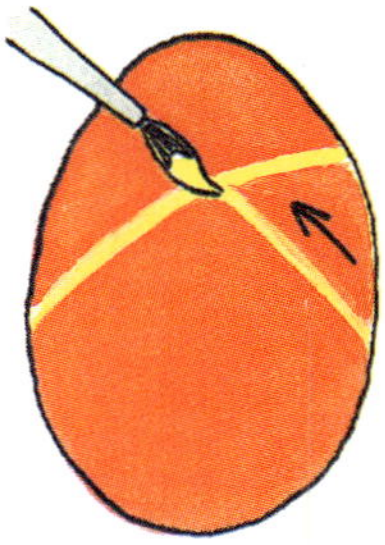

4 When the yellow paint is dry, use the fine-line brush to cover the top edge of the nail with white acrylic paint. Use the clear polish for the top coat.

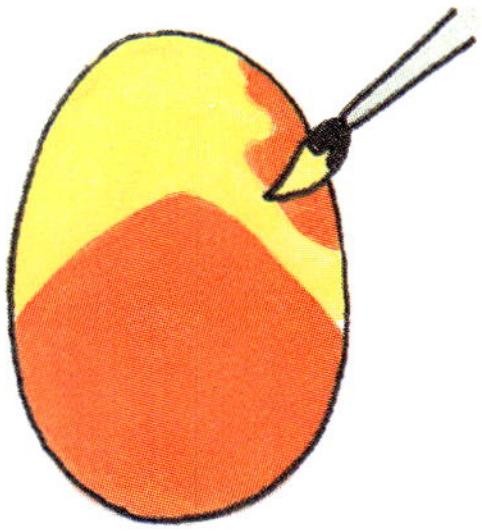

Face Paint Recipe

You'll need a parent to help you put this together.

- 2 tablespoons unflavored gelatin • measuring cups • cold water • mixing bowl
- spoon • saucepan • ¼ cup cornstarch • 4 tablespoons dishwashing liquid
- assorted colors of food coloring • empty plastic ice tray • paintbrush

1. Pour the gelatin and ⅓ cup cold water into a mixing bowl. Stir the mixture until it is dissolved, then set aside.
2. Next pour 2½ cups water into a saucepan and add the cornstarch. Heat the mixture until it boils. With a parent's help, stir continuously. Then reduce the heat so the mixture simmers. Continue stirring until the cornstarch is totally dissolved and fully thickened.
3. Now turn off the heat and stir in the gelatin mixture from Step 1.
4. Stir in the dishwashing liquid.
5. Once the mixture has cooled, spoon it evenly into the different compartments of the ice tray. Start adding drops of food coloring to each compartment, one color per compartment. The more drops you add, the richer your colors will look. You can also try mixing colors.
6. Use a thin paintbrush to apply it to your skin.

Scary Spiderweb & Black Cat Tattoo

Use water-soluble face paint crayons (available at beauty supply or costume stores), black eyeliner pencil, or the Face Paint Recipe (on page 43) to create a creepy-crawly web and a black cat on the tops of your feet or hands.

You Need

• water-soluble face paint crayon or face paint in black (or black eyeliner pencil), green, and red • paintbrush and plastic cup of water (if using our recipe for face paint)

Directions

Scary Spiderweb

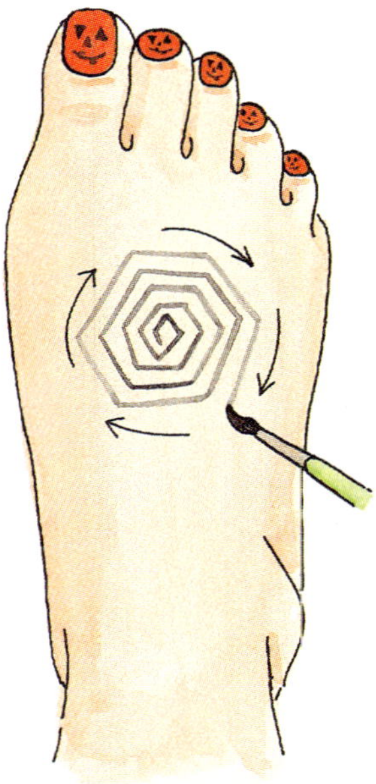

1. Use the top of your foot to form the center of your spiderweb. With black face paint or eyeliner pencil, draw a small diamond shape, as shown. Draw concentric stop-sign shapes around the diamond shape, as shown.

2. Draw a line from the center of your web outward and attach a spider to it. Fill in with black paint, but leave room for two red eyes.

3. Add more webs between your toes!

Black Cat Tattoo

1. With black face paint or eyeliner pencil, draw a crescent shape on the back of your hand.

2. At the right end of the crescent, paint on your cat's tail. Draw four legs at the bottom side of the crescent, as shown.

3 Draw a small triangle attached to the front part of the crescent. Add two more small triangles for ears.

4 Make two small green circles for eyes.

Pumpkin Toes

These happy jack-o'-lanterns perk up your toes!

You Need

• clear nail polish • orange nail polish • black acrylic paint
• white ceramic tray or palette paper • fine-line artist's brush • plastic cup of water
• green acrylic paint (optional)

Directions

1 Brush on a clear base coat. Let dry completely. Apply two coats of orange nail polish. Let your nails dry completely.

2 Put three or four drops of black acrylic paint on your tray or palette paper to form one large drop. Dip your fine-line brush in the water, then twirl the brush in the paint. Starting with your big toe, paint a tiny triangle, point facing upward, on the top right side of your nail. Paint a tiny triangle, point facing down, next to it. Paint a triangle for the nose. Paint a line for the mouth. If you have room, add two small squares, as shown.

3 Continue as shown with the rest of your toenails. You can vary your design by alternating the shapes of your pumpkin features and by using green paint for the shapes.

4 When your designs are completely dry, finish with a clear top coat.

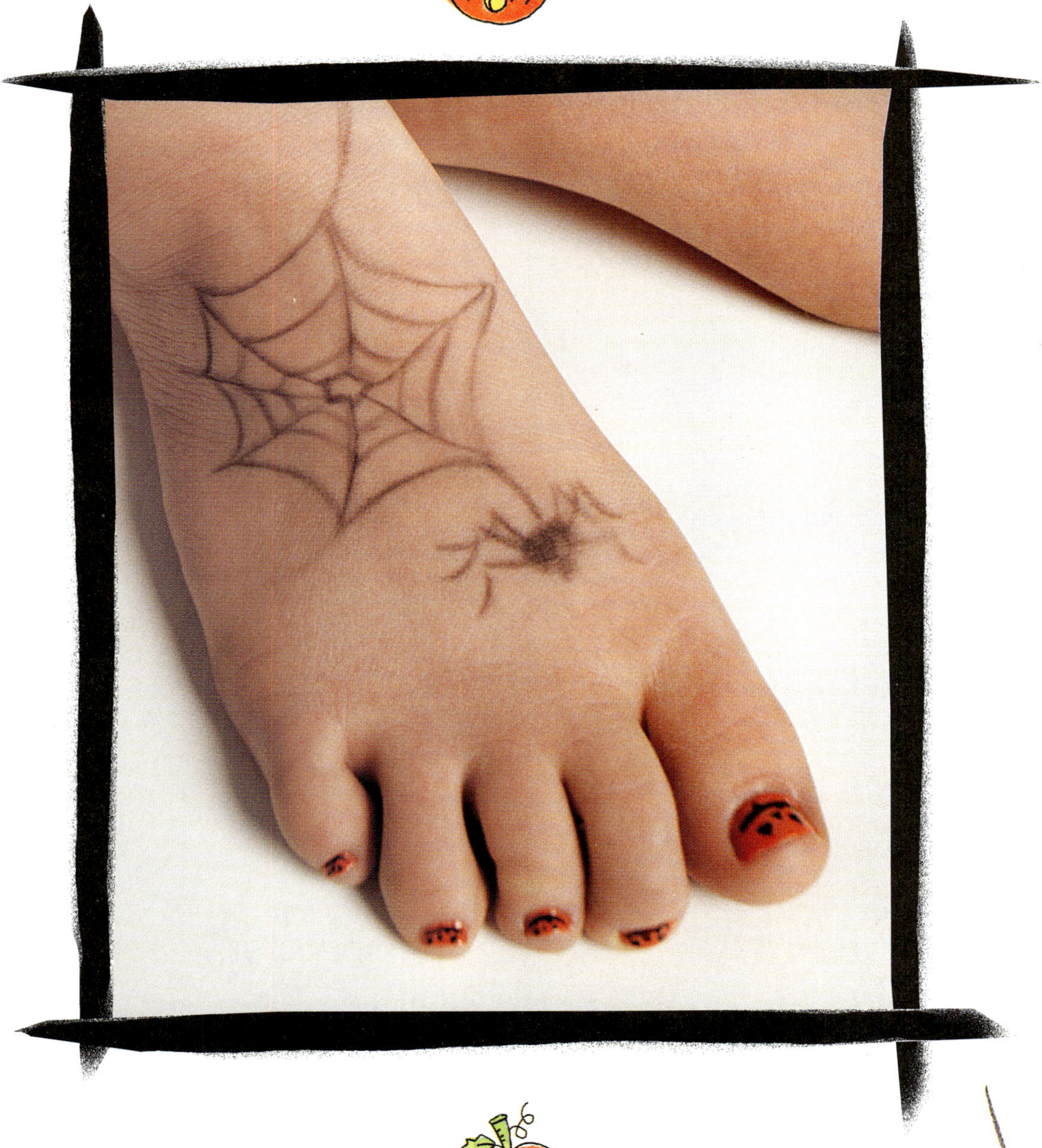

Snowflakes on the Fingertips

You'll want to snuggle in front of the fire with your best buddies to create this festive fingernail design.

You Need

• clear nail polish • blue and white acrylic paints • fine-line artist's brush • plastic cup of water • white ceramic tray or palette paper

Directions

1. Brush on a clear base coat. Let dry completely.

2. Apply two coats of blue acrylic paint, allowing each coat to dry. Clean your brush.

3. Put two to three small drops of white paint on your tray or palette paper. Dip your fine-line brush in the water, then roll the brush in the paint, making sure to cover all the bristles. Dip just the point of the brush in the paint again to make a fine point. Make a small dot in the center of the nail. Using the dot as your starting point, make a *V*. (Hint: Stroke up from the point.) Now paint an upside-down *V* from the same center point, this time stroking downward.

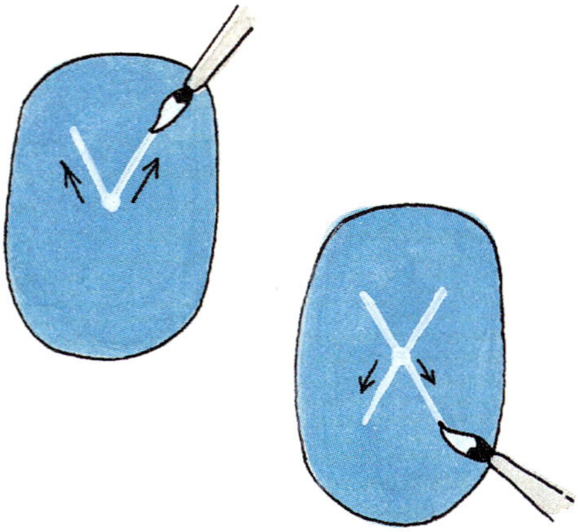

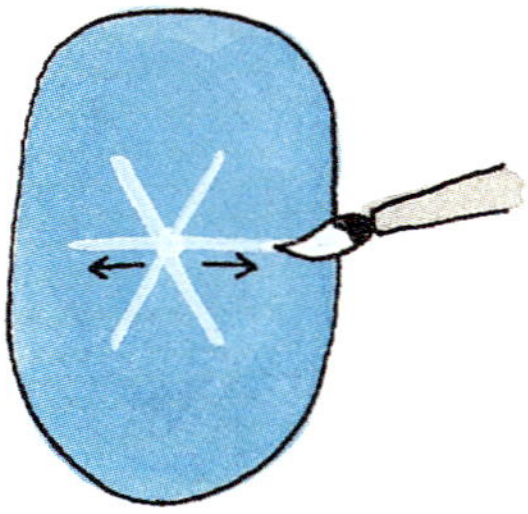

4. Paint a horizontal line through your center point, as shown.

5 Paint tiny *V*s from each end of your snowflake "star." When your snowflake is dry, seal with a clear top coat.

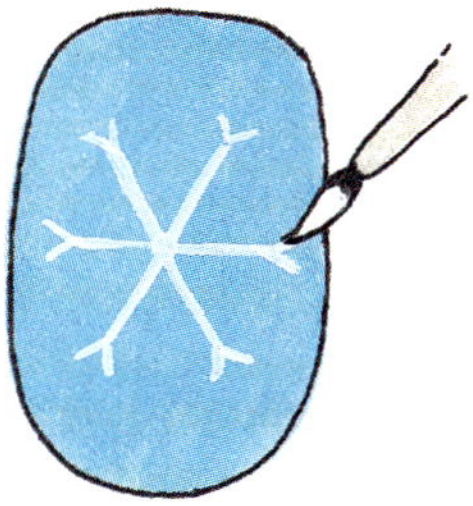

Go Glitter!

Instead of just white paint, add glitter to your snowflake. While the snowflake design is still wet, pour silver glitter over your nail. When your design is dry, seal with a clear top coat.

How to apply loose glitter to nail art:

1. **Fold a small square of white paper in half.**
2. **Pour a small amount of glitter in the crease of your paper.**
3. **While your design is still wet, carefully pour a bit of glitter onto the top of your entire nail. (As long as your base coat is dry, the glitter will stick only to the wet part of your design.)**
4. **Gently turn your hand over to dislodge any extra glitter.**

Candy Cane Toes

The design looks so much like real candy, you'll think you smell peppermint.

You Need

• clear nail polish • white and red acrylic paints • fine-line artist's brush • plastic cup of water • white ceramic tray or palette paper

Directions

1. Brush on a clear base coat. Let dry completely.

2. Put a couple drops each of white and red paint on the tray or palette paper. Apply two coats of white paint, allowing each coat to dry. Clean your brush.

3. Paint red diagonal stripes on your toenails. Finish with a clear top coat.

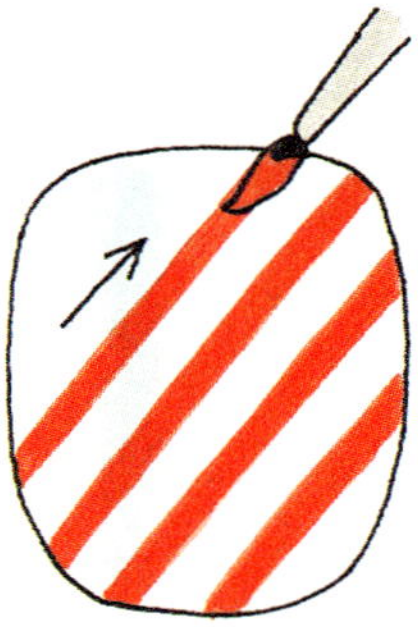

Peppermint Toe Rings

Use real candy! But don't stop with peppermint—use butterscotch suckers or sour balls in rainbow colors for every toe!

You Need

• peppermint candy (or any kind of hard candy with a flat side) • clear nail polish
• 2-inch piece of white knit nonroll elastic in 1/2-inch width (found in sewing stores)
• needle and white thread • white or craft glue

Directions

1. Unwrap your candy and paint the top of it with clear nail polish. Set aside to dry. Turn the candy over and paint the other side.

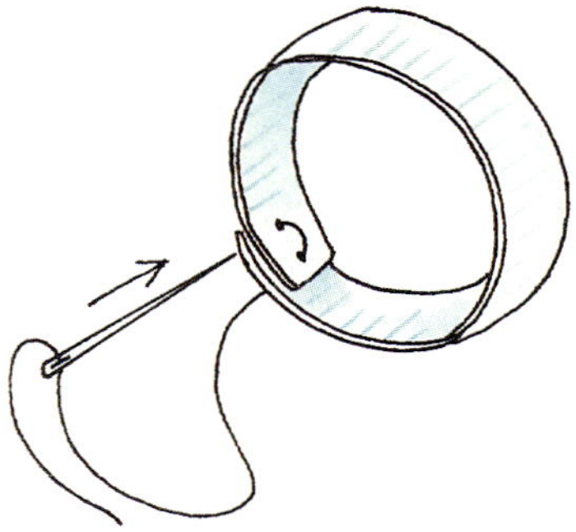

2. Wrap the elastic around your toe (or finger, if you want a finger ring) to make sure it will fit. (Make it a bit tight, as the elastic will stretch.) Sew ends of the elastic together with thread.

3. Put a dab of glue on the center of your candy and a bit on the elastic. Press the candy onto the elastic and let dry.

Wrap 'em Up!

In a hurry but want to look festive? Tie up each of your fingers with colored ribbons. Finish them off with a bow!

Hanukkah Fingers

Paint a blue Star of David on your nails to celebrate the Festival of Lights.

You Need

• clear nail polish • white nail polish • blue acrylic paint
• white ceramic tray or palette paper • fine-line artist's brush • plastic cup of water

Directions

1 Brush on a clear base coat. Let dry completely. Brush on two coats of white nail polish, allowing each coat to dry.

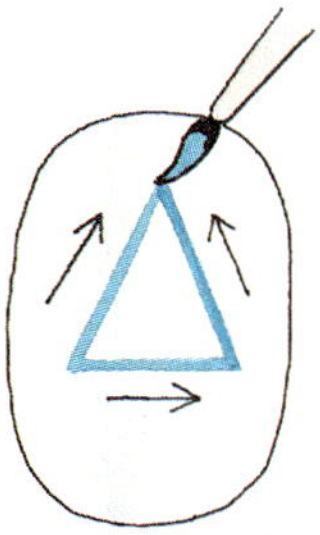

2 Put two or three small drops of blue paint on your tray or palette paper. Twirl your fine-line brush in the water, then the paint. Starting with your thumb, paint a triangle in the center of each nail.

3 Beginning with your thumb again, paint an upside-down triangle over the first one. If you want to, color in your star, as shown in the photo on page 55. Let dry.

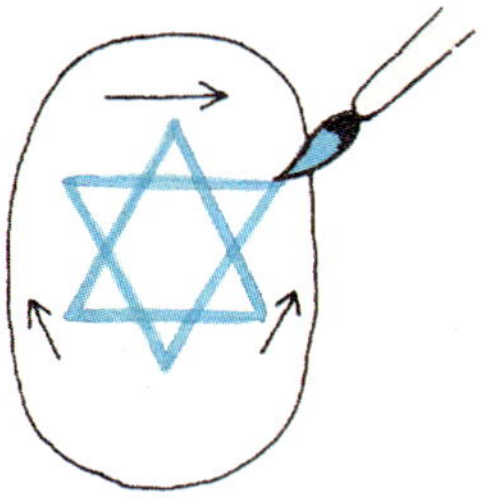

4 Finish with a clear top coat.

Teeny-Tiny Present Rings

Cute, wrapped present rings are a cinch to make. Wrap up a few for some holiday gifts!

You Need

• wrapping paper • two or three small dice, 1/4 inch to 1/2 inch in size • tape or glue • scissors • ruler • 1/8-inch-thick gold wire ribbon

Directions

1. Carefully wrap your dice, using a very small amount of tape or glue to secure the wrapping paper.

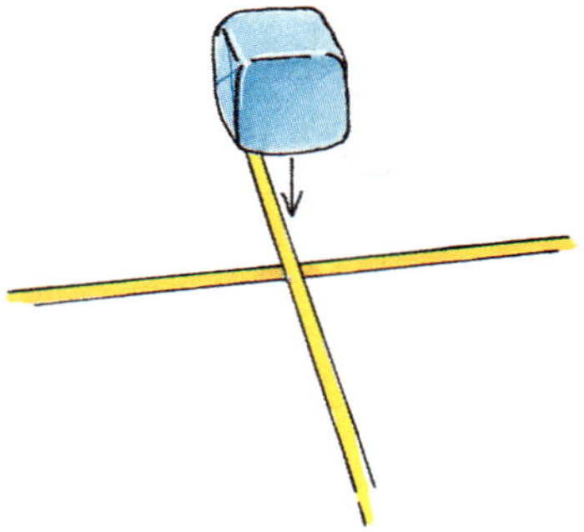

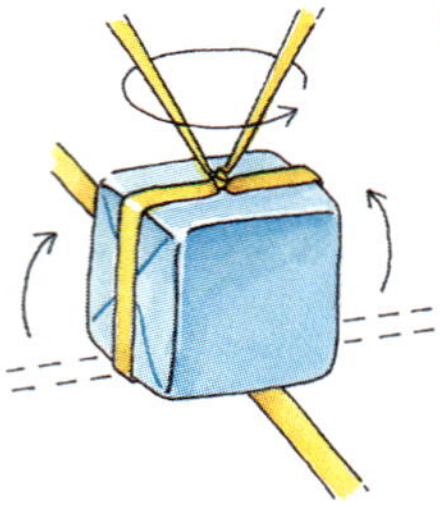

2. Cut two 8-inch pieces of the gold wire ribbon. Place one horizontally on a flat work surface. Lay the other one on top of it in a vertical direction, as shown. Lay the wrapped dice in the center of the ribbons where they meet.

3. Bring the sides of the horizontal piece up over the top of the present, twist, and bring back over the other side, as shown. Carefully flip the present over, twist the two ends together, and curl to make the bow. Cut off the excess.

4. Bring the remaining two sides from the other piece of ribbon down and twist.

5 To put the ring on your finger, twist the remaining two sides around your finger until snug. Trim off the excess. Twist again to keep it from unraveling.

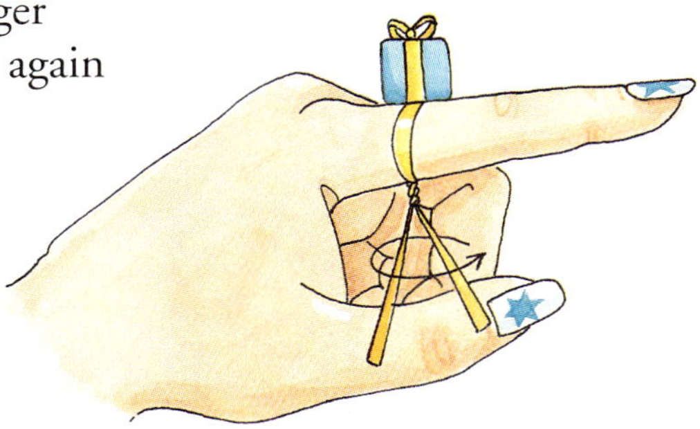

Stained Glass Nails

Dramatic!

You Need

• clear nail polish • gold glitter polish • black, green, blue, red, and pink acrylic paints • fine-line artist's brush • plastic cup of water • white ceramic tray or palette paper

Directions

1. Brush on a clear base coat. Let dry completely.

2. Brush on two coats of gold glitter polish. Let dry completely.

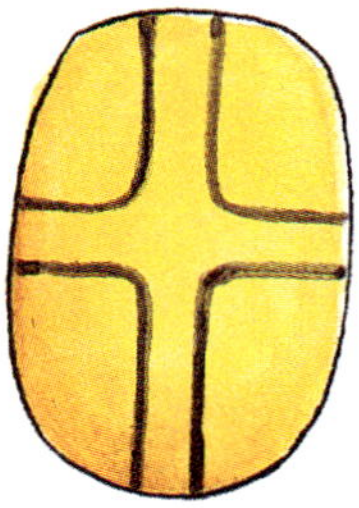

3. Put two small drops of black paint on your tray or palette paper. Dip your fine-line brush in the water, then twirl the brush in the paint. Beginning at the lower half of your nail, paint in four rectangular sections, as shown. Let dry. Clean your brush.

4. Set out two or three drops of green paint on your tray or palette paper. Dip your brush in the paint, then fill in the top left section of the nail. Let dry. Clean your brush.

5. Set out two or three drops of blue paint on your tray or palette paper. Dip your brush in the paint, then fill in the lower right section of the nail. Let dry. Clean your brush.

6. Set two or three drops of red paint on your tray or palette paper. Dip your brush in the paint, then fill in the top right section of the nail. Clean your brush.

7 Set out two or three drops of pink paint on your tray or palette paper. Dip your brush in the paint, then fill in the lower left section of the nail. Let dry completely.

8 Set out two drops of black paint on your tray or palette paper. Dip your brush in the water, then twirl it in the paint. Draw in more irregular shapes within each section, as shown. (If you have short nails, you may not have any more room for the design!)

9 When dry, fill in each of these shapes with other colors of your choice. Finish with a clear top coat.

Jingle All the Way

Thread tiny bells on yarn, thin curling ribbon, or wire ribbon for a musical bracelet.

You Need

- five or six small metal bells, preferably 9 mm in size (available at craft stores)
- 16-inch piece of yarn, $\frac{1}{8}$-inch curling ribbon, or wire ribbon • ruler • scissors

Directions

1. Tie a knot in the yarn or ribbon about $2\frac{1}{2}$ inches from one end. Then thread the yarn or ribbon through the bottom of the bell, and slide the bell up to the knot. Tie a knot at the other side of the bell to keep it from slipping. Tie another knot at a $\frac{1}{2}$-inch interval, and slip another bell onto the yarn or ribbon. Secure it with another knot. Continue threading bells onto the yarn or ribbon. Leave about $2\frac{1}{2}$ inches of yarn or ribbon at the other end.

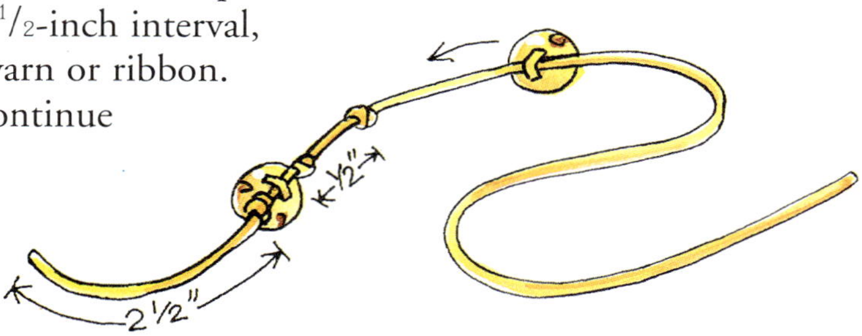

2. Wrap the bracelet around your wrist and secure the ends. Trim any excess yarn or ribbon.

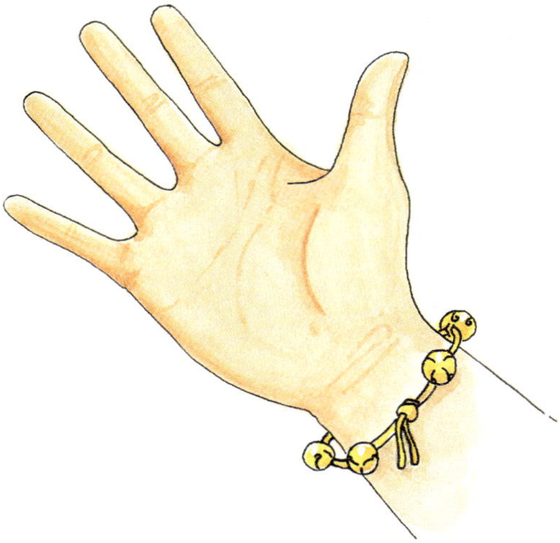

Bounty of Bracelets & Awesome Anklets

The next several crafts can be made to fit your wrist or ankle. Personalize each one to best fit your own style!

Toothbrush Teaser

Recycle your toothbrush for a beguiling bangle! Ask a parent to help.

You Need

• old toothbrush (the colored, transparent ones work best) • cup of very hot water • pliers • pot of boiling water • two oven mitts • tongs • large mug or glass • cold water

Directions

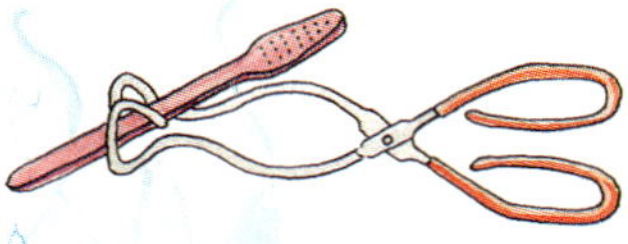

1. Dip your toothbrush, bristles down, in the cup of hot water for a few minutes to soften the bristles.

2. Pull out the bristles with pliers.

3. With a parent's help, boil water, then carefully place the toothbrush in the pot of boiling water. Leave the toothbrush in the still-boiling water for about five minutes.

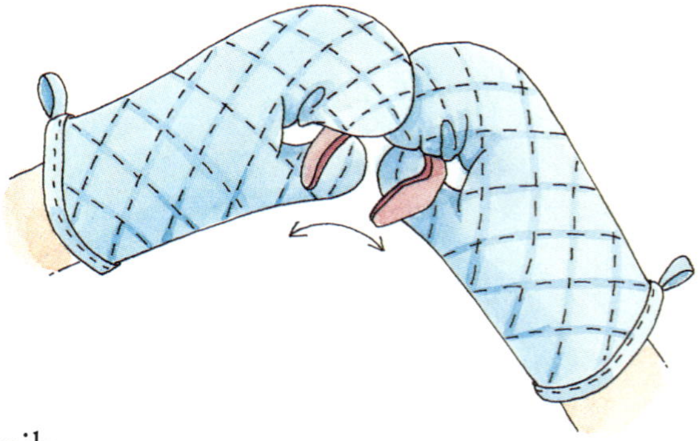

4. Put on oven mitts, then use the tongs to carefully remove the toothbrush from the water.

5. Using the mitts, bend the toothbrush into a circular shape. Put the toothbrush bangle into the bottom of the mug or glass to hold its shape. (If the toothbrush does not bend easily, put it back into the boiling water for a few more minutes.)

6 Let the bracelet cool thoroughly before removing it from the mug or glass. (Pour cold water into the mug or glass to help the cooling process along!)

Soccer Charm Bracelet

Show your team spirit with these tiny soccer-ball charms.

You Need

• quarter • Styrofoam® meat or deli tray, washed thoroughly • toothpick • scissors or utility knife • black permanent marker • embroidery needle • 8-inch piece of yarn

Directions

1 Place the quarter on the Styrofoam tray, and trace around it with a toothpick, scoring the Styrofoam. Make six or seven circles.

2 Use scissors or, with a parent's help, a utility knife to carefully cut out the quarter-sized circles.

3 Color in the soccer-ball diagram with your black permanent marker, as shown. Be sure to color in both sides of your Styrofoam circles.

4 Punch a hole in the top of each soccer ball with the embroidery needle or a toothpick.

5 String the balls on the yarn, then tie yarn around your wrist. Trim the excess yarn.

Denim Bead Bangle

Recycle old jeans for a new take on jelly-roll beads.

You Need

• paintbrush • five 1 1/2 x 10-inch triangles of denim • craft glue • 18- to 20-inch colored shoelace • wooden beads or colored beads • juice-box straw or pencil

Directions

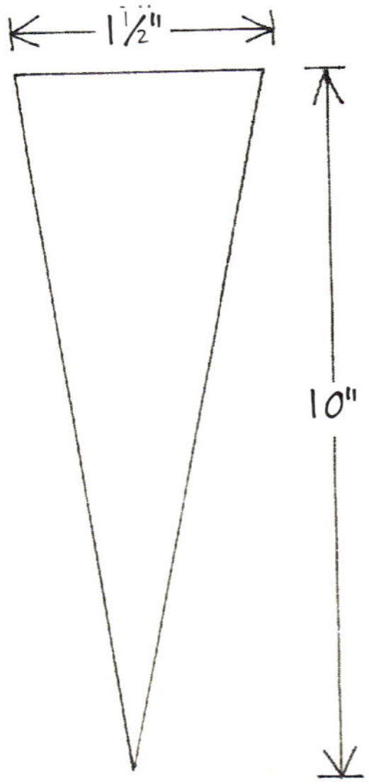

1. Brush one side of each denim triangle with glue.

2. Turn each triangle over and roll around the juice-box straw, pencil, or wooden end of the paintbrush.

3. Let the triangles dry (about two hours) and string them on the shoelace. Alternate one wooden or colored bead, then one denim bead. Tie a knot to fasten the anklet. Trim any excess shoelace.

Try This!

Vary the color of your denim beads by using stonewashed denim and dark denim, for example; or paint swirls on the fabric with fabric paint.

Industrial Tech Fashion

Found objects—from a parent's toolbox or hardware store—make a cool street-wear statement!

You Need

- assortment of rubber and metal washers, screws, nuts, bolts, etc.
- 18-inch piece of lanyard string

Directions

1. Simply string your hardware "charms" on the lanyard string, and tie to fasten! (If using screws, wind the string around the head of the screw a few times.)

Black-and-White Nail Art

A few final designs for you and your friends to do in just minutes. Get out your white and black acrylic paints for nail power in black and white!

Tic-Tac-Toe

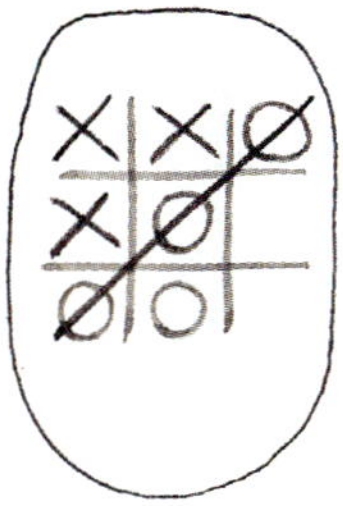

Show a new move on each nail!

Dominoes

Yin/Yang

Musical Notes

Peace Sign

Card Trick

You'll also need red paint for this study in black, white, and red.